THE STORY OF VIRTUE

Universal Lessons on How to Live

Joe Humphreys

The Liffey Press

Published by
The Liffey Press
Ashbrook House, 10 Main Street
Raheny, Dublin 5, Ireland
www.theliffeypress.com

© 2005 Joe Humphreys

A catalogue record of this book is
available from the British Library.

ISBN 1-904148-77-8

Illustrations by Frank Humphreys
(www.frankhumphreys.net; design@frankhumphreys.net)

Printed in Spain by GraphyCems.

CONTENTS

Acknowledgements vii

Introduction 1

1 *Empathy* 13

2 *Compassion* 29

3 *Charity* 45

4 *Self-Discipline* 59

5 *Loyalty* 75

6 *Audacity* 93

7 *Honesty* 107

8 *Humility* 123

9 *Tolerance* 135

10 *Wisdom* 155

11 *Work* 171

12 *Love* 185

13 *Justice* 203

14 *Mercy* 229

Epilogue 241

Index 251

ACKNOWLEDGEMENTS

Thanks to former tutors at the Department of Politics at University College Dublin, especially the audacious Fergal O'Connor, for lighting the spark of imagination. Thanks too to the various people — charitable and wise — who provided me with assistance and advice during the writing of this book. Any errors are, of course, my own. Much deserved praise goes to David Givens of The Liffey Press for courageously taking on such a risky project, and Brian Langan for his honesty and good humour in editing; I hope they get their reward! A special word of appreciation to my loyal brothers for their comments and debate, and in particular the industrious Frank for contributing illustrations. This book would not have been possible without the generosity of my wife, Emer, nor the tolerance of our baby daughter, Megan, who patiently endured many a trip to the library. A final mention for my parents, Richard and Deirdre: two better people I do not know.

For Megan

INTRODUCTION

In a world of religious diversity, where do you turn to for an answer to the question of how to live? To the religion of your birth (if you have one)? To an exotic new faith? To secularism or the cult of self-worship? With so many faiths on offer, it is hard to know who, or more precisely what, to believe.

A great temptation today is to follow fads, or engage in an endless cycle of "spirituality shopping". But changing your religion like you change your wardrobe is no recipe for enlightenment. Indecision is no foundation on which to build character. What one needs to navigate oneself through life's moral dilemmas is a firm grip on the wheel of one's conscience. What we need, in other words, is certainty. Instead we tend to have doubt. It is the downside of living in a choice-filled world.

Religious diversity, indeed, presents us with a challenge. But does it also create false choices in our lives? Must we choose between faith, on the one hand, and a moral and spiritual wilderness on the other, as claimed by many religious preachers? Must we rank different religions in order of superiority, as claimed by theological purists? Must we take

religious belief whole and uncensored or leave religion altogether, as claimed by many secularists?

The Story of Virtue argues that we have created a false division between religious and secular traditions, and that this
false division permeates not just our private lives but our
public discourse. It is commonly believed that the world's
major religions are incompatible with one another where, in
fact, they share much in common — more than many religious leaders will freely admit. In particular, there exists between the faiths a shared appeal to men and women to
cultivate certain human qualities — call them virtues if you will
— like compassion, honesty, mercy, loyalty and wisdom —
virtues which can also be admired from a secular perspective.

A total of fourteen virtues, drawn from the world's major
religious traditions, are examined in this book. Some are more
closely associated with particular traditions than others. Love,
for instance, is commonly linked with Christianity, justice with
Islam, self-discipline with Buddhism, and audacity with Judaism.
All the virtues discussed, however, are celebrated by a combination of traditions to a greater or lesser degree.

It should be noted that when we speak of virtues we
speak of human qualities that are deliberately cultivated
rather than sustained naturally or innately in men and
women. That is not to discount the possibility that you are
born with particular virtues. However, "being virtuous" is a
conscious decision, or learnt response, whether it translates
as tending to the virtues you already have, or developing ones
you don't. As such, "virtue" should be distinguished from the
narrow perception of the concept that exists within some
organised religions, and moral philosophies. Among other

things, the "virtue" referred to in this book encapsulates both positive and negative ethics: both "refraining from harm" and "doing good". As argued in the chapter on compassion, no other account of "virtue" makes sense.

The traditions explored in *The Story of Virtue* include the monotheisms of Christianity, Islam and Judaism and the looser faiths of Hinduism, Confucianism and Buddhism.[1] Naturally, this book cannot claim to tell readers everything about such belief systems but it seeks to capture the essence of them — by using a very specific methodology. Religion is here scrutinised, not so much through doctrine or theology but through narrative — the moral stories, fables and parables handed down through generations.

Some of these stories are factual, others not so. But all have something to teach us by illustrating how to face life's challenges: suffering or success, ignorance or knowledge, good fortune or ill, and so on. Importantly, we delve into secular as well as religious literature, identifying stories and myths that inspire people who belong to no organised religion. Some of the tales in this book, therefore, feature prophets, saints and divinities, while others feature "ordinary folk" acting virtuously, or meeting an ideal of moral excellence, as judged by religious or secular standards. In that sense, the various episodes recalled here could be collectively described as "stories of the divine".

Some people may question the validity of this approach and say that stories have a place in religion but only in support of accepted scripture. However, stories not only pre-date such scripture; they provide the medium through which it is understood. Before the New Testament was written, for example, Jesus told parables on how to live a good life, and before we can understand what the New Testament means we must tell the story of Jesus. Similarly, up to 2,000 years before anyone called themselves a "Hindu" (a term introduced by the British in India at the end of the eighteenth century) morality tales like the *Mahabharata* circulated in the Indian sub-continent. Gurus who teach what is today called "Hinduism" continue to draw on such tales, knowing that without them their teachings would make no sense.

Thus, the stories retold in this book are, literally, timeless. They were composed not as historical documents but as lessons for life. While they come from a variety of religious traditions, they were often written or formulated before those traditions had solidified into the "faiths" that we know today. In other words, they were often composed before religious intermediaries — clergy, spiritual leaders, and the like — began to replace them with legal texts of a narrower and more prescriptive nature. By returning to these stories we can reclaim a lost wisdom that has been covered up for generations by theological "scholarship" and obfuscation. In short, we can return to the true spirit of religious traditions, and discover what they mean for us today.

As well as being a useful guide to understanding faith-based traditions, story-telling is a fruitful means of answering questions of an ethical nature — by providing a practical example of the "moral" at stake. To read a tale of virtue is, of course, no substitute for meeting the virtuous in person, let alone practising virtue oneself. But perhaps it is the next best thing. Because they are free, or freer, of technical jargon than doctrinal tracts, morality tales speak to a universal audience.

By retelling them, furthermore, we are following in the time-honoured tradition of Moses, Muhammad, Confucius and many other moral and spiritual educators. From the Buddhist *Jakata* tales to the episodic *hadiths* of Islam, and from *Adam and Eve* to *Aesop's Fables*, story-telling has been a central part of religious instruction.

It should be said that *The Story of Virtue* is aimed at both readers with a religion and those without. The latter tend to dismiss religion at best as a cultural oddity, and at worst a dangerous source of division in the world. But regardless of one's view of faith, and whether it is a force for good or bad, one cannot avoid coexisting with "believers" unless one does away with "belief". As someone who is not a member of any religion but who accepts that people have a right to freedom of conscience, I have no choice but to try to accommodate my non-worshipping with the worshipping of others. That accommodation starts with listening and learning.

In an increasingly polarised world, religious and secular groupings tend to restrict themselves to reading and retelling stories that affirm their own particularly preconceived ideas. Each group tends to believe that its own faith, whatever it may be, has a monopoly on wisdom; that no one knows virtue better than it does. *The Story of Virtue* demonstrates, however, that morality tales from across the religious divide share many themes, story-lines, and most importantly, lessons for all of humanity. In this way, it challenges not only religious believers who see no value in traditions other than their own but secularists who think they have nothing to learn from stories of the divine. By focusing on common virtues, *The Story of Virtue* points to a universal human ethic that largely predates, and perhaps overcomes, factional religious teaching. In the process, it suggests that, in our own lives, we can find certainty on questions of morality despite competition between organised faiths.

That is not, of course, to say all religious traditions have the same approach to matters ethical. For a start, a virtue that is prized by one religion may barely register with another. Different virtues are understood differently by each faith. Western religions like Islam and Christianity, for example, believe justice to demand vigorous efforts aimed at creating a fair society, while eastern faiths like Hinduism and Buddhism believe it to entail a more cautious and perhaps more pacifistic approach. Moreover, different religious practitioners are virtuous for different reasons. In accordance with orthodox teaching, Christians and Muslims see virtue as an escape-route from eternal damnation, while Buddhists and Hindus see it as a pathway to enlightenment. However, *The Story of Virtue* claims there is enough common ground between the faiths to suggest that agreement is possible on how people should, in a very fundamental way, interact with one another.

In this sense, the book is political as well as personal. It contests the modern hypothesis that religion is an inevitable source of conflict in the world. On the surface, it seems religion creates tensions. Fundamentalism is on the rise. Christians, Muslims, Buddhists, Jews, believers and non-believers are speaking to each other less and distrusting each other more. A clash of civilisations has been predicted. But it need not be so. *The Story of Virtue* suggests that dialogue, and even agreement, between the world's major faiths is possible if we ask the right question, namely: "How should we live?" Instead of trying to answer this question, religious leaders and other participants in inter-faith dialogue tend to concentrate on questions that are guaranteed to produce division, like "What is the nature of God?", "Is there an afterlife?" or, to take a highly charged issue from Christianity, "Does the Eucharist in Catholic Mass contain the 'real presence' of Christ?". Agreement will only be reached on these questions if one eradicates religious difference. But agreement is possible, or so it is here argued, on a universal human ethic, notwithstanding difference between the faiths.

An underlying question which religious leaders and practitioners need to ask themselves is whether religion is, above all, a guide for living rather than an explanation for human existence; whether it is more a matter of practice than belief. Whether Wittgenstein was right when he said: "Christianity is not a doctrine . . . but a description of something that actually takes place in human life."[2] Or whether Nietzsche was correct when he wrote: "It is false to the point of absurdity to see in a 'belief', perchance the belief in redemption through Christ, the distinguishing characteristic of the Christian: only Christian practice, a life such as he who died on the Cross lived, is Christian."[3]

If one takes what both authors say about Christianity to be true for all faiths it alters radically the prospects of inter-faith dialogue. If the test of a good Christian, a good Muslim or a good Jew is not abstract belief but (real) practice — if it is, in essence, the life one leads, and the virtue one demonstrates — then Christians, Muslims and Jews can speak with a common language, namely the language of virtue. And they can speak with a common purpose, namely the promotion of virtue.

Some readers may wish to place this book within a particular philosophical category, in which case it could be seen as a return to "Aristotelian" thought in the sense of viewing morality through the prism of virtue. This approach is described today as "virtue theory" to distinguish it from two other main types of moral philosophy, namely deontology, which deals mainly with rights and duties; and utilitarianism, which measures actions by their impact on collective happiness.[4] Virtue theory is typically traced back to Aristotle. However, Aristotle was merely the first thinker to formulate the principles behind the theory for a western audience. As the ethicist Alasdair MacIntyre points out, virtue theory dates at least as far back as the Heroic Eras of the Greeks, Norse and Celts; albeit some of the virtues they advocated, like physical strength and battle-field bravery, are less celebrated today. By speaking of virtues, or formulating a contemporary virtue theory, we are, therefore, getting back to our moral roots. We are, moreover, returning to a language which MacIntyre and others have cogently argued is best suited to resolving competing value-claims today.[5]

Coming back to the story-telling nature of this book, a word of warning should be added: while readers may gain direct access through stories to the moral vision of different traditions, there is no guarantee of "correct" understanding. This is inevitable, given the divergence of opinion within traditions about the meaning of texts and ethical standards. The *Bhagavad-Gita*, for example, the most sacred text of Hinduism, which tells the story of the warrior God Arjuna wrestling with his conscience before entering the field of battle, was read in polar-opposite ways by two important figures in

Indian history: Gandhi and his assassin. While "the Mahatma" viewed the tale as a parable of non-violence, the Indian separatist who murdered him saw it as a defence of the reverse.[6]

In reading the stories in this book, therefore, you should draw your own conclusions, and in doing so feel free to disagree with particular interpretations that are offered. Indeed, that is the only way to read this book if you wish to avoid perhaps another round of vacuous spirituality shopping. The stories here told should not be seen as dead art, or precious literature, to comfort you in retirement; they were not composed for that purpose. Rather, they should be seen as live arrows fired to prick your conscience. You may decide to fend off each arrow, but at least allow yourself to be challenged by them.

Some will refuse the challenge, perhaps believing they have nothing to learn from religious traditions, or perhaps believing their own faith tells them all they need to know. Their rejectionism reflects that of partitionists on a global stage who balk at the notion of a universal human ethic.

Significantly, there are those at both conservative and liberal extremes who reject the idea of virtue to start with. Religious fundamentalists argue that nothing counts but membership of the "correct" faith. There is, in their view, just one "virtue": righteousness — something which allows for atrocities to be carried out in God's name.

On the liberal extreme, meanwhile, a strand of thought attacks virtue for its connotations of social conformity or restraint. To be virtuous is to be sanctimonious or judgemental, according to one fashionable relativist creed. In the guilt-free world in which some like to live, virtue hails from

an austere, controlling era. Moreover, as it belongs to the
relatively unscientific world of ethics, virtue can be dismissed
as a fantasy. At best, it has meaning for the individual who
believes in it. But it has no place in public discourse, so the
argument runs, as it is part of a necessarily divisive and contradictory theoretical framework.

Virtue is, thus, attacked from both "Far Left" and "Far
Right", and inevitably so — because virtue is a challenge to
extremism. Each virtue is a trough between two extremes, or
"a mean that lies between two vices", as Aristotle said. Courage is a valley between cowardice and rashness, modesty between licentiousness and self-pity. No virtue exists without a
pair of competing vices. Nor does a theory of virtue exist
without two opposing modes of thought. *The Story of Virtue*
stands in opposition to the preachers of both righteousness
and irresponsibility, advocating a philosophy between the extremes of religious fundamentalism and secular amorality.

The threat of over-simplification is great with a project
like this. It is almost unfathomable to think of comparing in
such a short volume the moral perspective of such rich and
diverse traditions as Christianity, Islam, Chinese and Indian
philosophy, and Judaism, among other faiths. Isolationists argue that we can't compare. "We" are different to "them",
they claim; "our" values are irreconcilable with "theirs".
Thus, the world is reduced to a clash of faiths, where "you
are with us or against us".

Even among those who try to argue for inter-faith dialogue there is pessimism about the process. "It is not the case
that all religions are the same," wrote the religious historian
Wilfred Cantwell Smith. "If a philosopher ask[s] (anhistori-

cally) what they all have in common, he or she either finds the answer to be 'nothing', or finds that they all have in common something so much less than each has separately so as to distort or to evacuate the individual richness and depth and sometimes grotesqueness of actual religious life."[7]

Do the world's major faiths have "so much less" in common than in contrast? Yes, if one concentrates on rituals, customs and theological nuances; and some will argue these are the defining aspects of all religions. But what if one looks instead at how people from different faiths actually behave? What do they aspire to? And what sorts of actions do they applaud?

In advancing the case for a global ethic, *The Story of Virtue* should be read with a critical eye. The book seeks to prompt you, the reader, to ask yourself what it means to be good, and to see whether your answers tally with those provided by different faiths. By pointing the way to a shared understanding of virtue, *The Story of Virtue* does not wish to eradicate differences between traditions. Rather, it aims at encouraging you to ask, where differences occur, "How significant are they?" and "Can they be overcome?"

By so talking up the prospects of inter-faith dialogue, one is arguably demonstrating the virtue of hope or, alternatively, the vice of naïvety. A fine line runs between the two, as readers of this book should bear in mind.

Is it hopeful or naïve to imagine a universal human ethic? Read on and decide for yourself.

Endnotes

---

1 Three of the traditions examined in this book (Hinduism, Buddhism and Confucianism) tend to be called "eastern", and the other three "western", although western is something of a misnomer as Christianity, Islam and Judaism were all founded in the Middle East. "Abrahamic" is an alternative title for such traditions, given that Abraham is a common "father of the prophets" for Christians, Muslims and Jews. It should be pointed out that when we speak in this book of Hinduism, Buddhism, Confucianism, Christianity, Islam and Judaism we speak of them in the main as "traditions" rather than "faiths" or "religions" in recognition of the fact that we are delving beyond factional religious teaching to discover something essential in their collective heritage. We also avoid a somewhat distracting and convoluted argument about what exactly constitutes a religion, and whether any of the traditions above actually meet the criteria of one.

2 Wittgenstein, L. quoted in Monk, R. (1991), *Ludwig Wittgenstein: The Duty of Genius*, London: Vintage, p. 376.

3 Nietzsche, F. (1920), "The Anti-Christ", 39, as quoted in Monk, R., *op. cit.*, p. 122.

4 One academic neatly summarises the division thus: "Deontological systems of ethics typically emphasise rules, commandments, and precepts, which impose obligations we have a duty to fulfil. By contrast, utilitarianism . . . seeks justification in the future through the good consequences that are expected to flow from the performance of an act. . . . Virtue ethics is something of a middle way between the other two and tends to look both to the past and future for justification. According to virtue ethics . . . what is of primary importance in ethics are neither pre-existing obligations nor pleasant outcomes, but the development of character so that a person becomes habitually and spontaneously good." Keown, D. (2005) *Buddhist Ethics*, Oxford University Press, p. 22–3.

5 The argument is made at length in MacIntyre, A. (1981), *After Virtue*, London: Duckworth.

6 Fashing, D.J. and Dechant D. (2001), *Comparative Religious Ethics: A Narrative Approach*, Massachusetts: Blackwell Publishing, p. 124.

7 Cantwell Smith, W. (1989), *Towards a World Theology: Faith and the Comparative History of Religion* (Library of Philosophy and Religion), London: Macmillan, p. 5.

EMPATHY

There was once a young prince called Siddhartha Gautama who grew up with the best of everything. So sheltered was his life that he never once left his father's palace until close to his thirtieth birthday.

It was then, one morning, that he called his charioteer, and asked him to prepare for a trip into the forest. The two ventured outside the gates and down a twisting path where the prince saw an old man resting on a walking stick. "What is wrong with that man?" the prince asked. "He is old," the charioteer replied. "Everyone gets old sometime."

The next morning the prince took another journey from the palace — this time further into the countryside. There, he came across a man lying on the side of the road and groaning. "What's happening?" the prince asked. His charioteer replied: "The man is ill. We all fall ill sometime."

The following day the prince went out again, and on this occasion, encountered a group of people weeping as they trailed behind a funeral procession. Looking at the corpse, Siddhartha asked: "Is that man

sleeping? And why are those people crying?" To
which his charioteer replied: "The man is dead. We
will all die sometime."

On the fourth morning, the prince took a final trip
outside of the palace gates, and travelled deeper into
the forest until he came across an itinerant monk
who was meditating. The man was dressed in rags but
peaceful and content. "Who is that?" the prince
asked. His charioteer replied: "He is a Holy man who
has seen the suffering of the world — ageing, illness
and death — and has abandoned worldly goods for an
ascetic life."

Siddhartha remarked: "I will do the same." And so
the young prince, who would become the Buddha, left
the palace to begin his new vocation.[1]

Empathy is perhaps the most fundamental of all virtues. Yet it
is also the most difficult to define. On a surface level, it seems
like no virtue at all but rather a chance event, or involuntary
action, to which no moral significance can be attached. Take
the opening tale, *The Story of the Four Sights*, a founding myth
of Buddhism. Was it not a fluke that the Buddha was moved
to comtemplation by the various scenes of human suffering
which he had come across? No conscious decision appeared
to have been made to associate himself with the plight of
others. Rather, the Buddha seemed to empathise despite
himself, and in that case what credit is due?

The answer lies in the story's context, for the Buddha's
moral awakening did not come from nowhere. In the Buddhist tradition, Prince Siddhartha's was the final life that the
Buddha led before obtaining enlightenment. In accordance
with the faith's doctrine of reincarnation, the Buddha had

died thousands of times previously and on each occasion was reborn into an existence more virtuous than the last. The prince himself, while sheltering from the woes of the world, was renowned for his sensitive nature and caring attitude towards other beings. He was, in other words, amenable to being influenced by the sight of human suffering. He had done the moral groundwork to allow himself empathise.

Siddhartha's response, therefore, may appear to have been instinctive. But it was not necessarily inevitable. Like anyone who empathises with another, the future Buddha repressed certain thoughts; thoughts like "this person who is suffering is not me"; thoughts which aid detachment. That such thoughts invade the human mind explains why the sight of a starving child moves one person to tears but not another.

The Buddha thus made a choice of sorts, the same choice made by anyone who empathises. In dramatic terms, one could summarise it as "letting oneself cry". While the Buddha did not actually shed tears in *The Story of the Four Sights*, his weeping could be heard "off-stage".[2] It was, moreover, reciprocated when the Buddha himself reached the end of his life, and lay down to die between two *sal* trees. It is recalled:

> Seeing his friend and teacher so weak and ill Ananda [the Buddha's cousin and personal assistant] was filled with grief.
>
> "What shall we do without you?" he said, and began to sob bitterly . . .
>
> "Remember the teaching," [the Buddha replied.] "Everything changes and passes away. Now go and strive diligently."[3]

Both episodes tell us something about the importance of empathy to Buddhism but also something about the virtue itself. To empathise is to acknowledge, in a profound way, that life is transient. It is to remember, as the Buddha said, that "everything changes and passes away".

Other faiths are equally forceful on the point. "Remember death abundantly," said 'Umar Ibn 'Abd al-'Aziz, one of the earliest "righteous caliphs" of Islam.[4] "Death is a fact and people should not forget it," an Islamic commentator adds. "By remembering it, we can improve our morality and our behaviour."[5]

But mindfulness of death is not just advocated by religions. It is a theme of morality tales stretching back to pagan times. In *The Epic of Gilgamesh*, from the ancient civilisation of Mesopotamia, a boastful and boorish warrior (Gilgamesh) was shown to have matured into a wise and sensitive prince once he had appreciated, and come to terms with, his own mortality. The turning point for Gilgamesh was when his friend Enkidu fell ill and died. The once unflappable and reckless hero was reduced to a blubbering mess, weeping over the body of his friend for six days and seven nights. "Am I not like him [Enkidu]? Must I lie down too, never to rise, ever again?" he whined before taking off on a voyage to try to find some answers.[6] Eventually, the penny dropped when Gilgamesh met the sage Utnapishtim who confirmed: "Death is inevitable . . . at some time, both for Gilgamesh and for a fool."[7]

The story confirms that when you cry for another you also, and perhaps even in the first instance, cry for yourself. Empathy, however, is not self-pity. The virtue implies that when you "let yourself cry" you do so with a purpose. To empathise, in short, is to appreciate something essential about the nature of human existence, and then to allow that appreciation shape one's moral outlook and influence one's future actions. It is, for example, to do what Leo Tolstoy did when he read the following Hindu fable:

> The human condition is . . . like that of a man who, fleeing from a furious beast, falls into a well and is held from dropping into the jaws of a devouring dragon below only by clinging to a bush that will, he sees, presently inevitably give way, since it is being nibbled at by two mice, one white and one black, that go round and round and slowly but relentlessly gnaw at its roots. The two mice are day and night; the bush, which tastes sweet at first but soon loses its savour, is one's worldly position; man knows that he or she must in due course die.[8]

Reading the story had a similar influence on Tolstoy as witnessing the "four sights" had on the future Buddha. As Tolstoy recalled in his *Confession*, the fable crystallised his understanding of the world, and man's place within it, thereby causing him to renounce his previous writings and dedicate the remainder of his life to the performance of good works in accordance with the Christian faith. Of the story, he wrote, "this is no fable. It is a real unanswerable truth."[9]

Here, again, we see how empathy is a far from universal reaction to the identification of suffering. Just as the sight of a starving child will move some people to tears but not others, the realisation that death comes to everyone will bring about a moral awakening in but a select few. After all, how many people will see the "real unanswerable truth" — a life-

altering, religious truth — in the Hindu story above, and how
many will rather turn the page, unaffected?

The crucial point on which all traditions agree is that everyone is capable of empathising. Most faiths qualify this and
say only *human beings* are capable of empathising.[10] According
to Christian teaching, for instance, humans are unique in the
animal kingdom in each having a conscience. In a similar vein,
Confucianism speaks of *jen*, or "human-heartedness", as "the
distinguishing characteristic of man".[11] No animal has *jen*,
which is likened to a moral compass that many people care-
lessly ignore. As Mencius, a prominent disciple of Confucius,
explained: "That whereby man differs from the birds and
beasts is but slight. The mass of people cast it away, whereas
the superior man preserves it."[12]

This human/animal dichotomy is reinforced in morality
tales from across the globe. One story from Islamic lore recounts how the Prophet Muhammad encountered on his
travels a camel who had been mistreated by his owner, an
"infidel" named Abu Masudi:

> The camel described at length various torments he
> had been put through, and the Prophet "sank down,
> weeping with compassion" before sending the animal
> to graze in a pasture. Muhammad then went to Abu
> Masudi to complain about his cruelty. The Prophet
> persuaded the man to return with him to the camel to
> answer the allegations in person. But on their way
> they passed a gazelle which was tied up in irons in a
> narrow pen. The animal explained that it had been
> captured four days previously after giving birth to two
> baby gazelles whom it had yet to feed. "I am worried
> to death about them. I am not crying for myself, but

for my two babies, who are starving in the forest," the gazelle continued. When Muhammad heard these words: "His heart could not bear it, he sobbed — and blubbered." The Prophet persuaded the owner of the gazelle to release the animal so it could breastfeed its offspring. The gazelle kept its word to Muhammad by returning after the deed was done. So moved by the act, the owner agreed to release the animal. But Abu Masudi was unwavering, and still insisted on hearing his camel's complaints. Only when this was done did he relent, and admit his guilt, agreeing to release the camel and to live piously ever after.[13]

Leaving aside the question of whether animals should be treated as "humanely" as human beings (a question that will be addressed in the next chapter), the story suggests that man should at least empathise with other living creatures. By contrasting the weeping prophet with the stony-hearted animal owners, it teaches that failure to relate the suffering of others is not just inhumane but inhuman. By failing to empathise, one denies one's own humanity.

Another story from Islam which celebrates empathy is *The Tragedy of Kerbala*, a historic legend surrounding the death of Hussein, the Prophet Muhammad's grandson. Hussein, known as the first Imam of Shi'ism, refused to submit to the authority of the rival Umayyad Caliph and was thereby drawn into war. He tried to avoid a direct confrontation for he knew he would be hopelessly outnumbered in battle. However, the Caliph tracked him down, eventually cornering him in an exposed plain near the River Euphrates. Each time Hussein ran out to fetch water for his thirsting family he was met with a hail of arrows, one of which came through the door of his tent and

killed a child in his arms. Eventually, Hussein himself was murdered — struck by so many arrows that he was propped
above the ground when he fell from his horse.

What, you might ask, has the story got to do with empathy? Well, in the Shi'a tradition, the story is never told without the accompaniment of great bouts of weeping. An
outside observer described the scene at a Shi'a festival:

> . . . the audience bursts into loud, unrestrained sob-
> bing, moaning and slapping of the forehead and beat-
> ing of chests. The words . . . are carefully chosen by
> the narrator to maximise the sentiments and emo-
> tions associated with filial and parental love which are
> strongly felt by each of the participants.[14]

Muslims who join in the "unrestrained sobbing" follow the
example of Zaynu'l-'Abidin, Hussein's only surviving son of
the massacre, who is known to some Islamic scholars as "the
greatest weeper in history". Whenever water was brought to
him in the years after the tragedy, Zaynu'l-'Abidin reportedly
wept, crying: "My father died thirsty at Kerbala".[15]

Four other "great weepers" can be found in Islamic history, according to one collection of Muslim literature. They
are: "Adam who cried for three hundred years, repenting his
fall; Noah, who wept when he learnt that all the children of
Adam would be drowned in the Flood, except he himself, his
wife and children; Jacob who wept for Joseph; and Fatima
who wept for her father [Muhammad]."[16]

To this list we could add Jesus who, according to Muslim
tradition, "stood long and wept bitterly" on the night of his
conversion to Islam. As the story goes:

> Jesus left the temple and the city and headed for the
> hills. He was outraged and consumed by [ardour] for
> the truth. His face became paler with grief over the
> dominance of evil in the world. . . . His tears flowed,
> streamed down his cheeks falling to the earth. . . .
> The matter was set, Jesus turned the page from a life
> of ease to a page of reflection and worship. His jour-
> ney of struggle and pain started — a journey of calling
> people to Allah to a new kingdom where evil cannot
> destroy goodness.[17]

While Jesus doesn't cry so freely in the Bible, the Christian
son of God does weep on a handful of occasions. All significantly relate to dying or death. In John's Gospel, Jesus famously sheds tears over the death of Lazarus;[18] in Luke he
weeps over the destruction of Jerusalem;[19] while, in Hebrews, it is recorded: "In his early life on earth Jesus made his
prayers and requests with loud cries and tears to God, who
could save him from death."[20] Jesus is also commonly said to
have "wept" in the Garden of Gethsemane ahead of his arrest
and crucifixion. In Matthew, it is said: "Grief and anguish
overcame him . . . He threw himself face downwards on the
ground, and prayed, 'My Father, if it is possible take this cup
of suffering from me!'"[21]

While crying doesn't necessarily imply empathy, the two
often feature together in religious stories. A recurrent theme
of Christian literature is religious conversion through cathar-
tic weeping rather than a cool, calculated examination of the
facts. In his *Confessions*, Augustine recalled that the moment
of spiritual departure in his life came while he was sitting with
his friend Alypius in their garden in Milan. He wrote:

I probed the hidden depths of my soul and wrung its pitiful secrets from it, and when I mustered them all before the eyes of my heart, a great storm broke within me, bringing with it a great deluge of tears. I stood up and left Alypius so that I might weep and cry to my heart's content, for it occurred to me that tears were best shed in solitude. . . . So I stood up and left where we had been sitting, utterly bewildered. Somehow I flung myself down beneath a fig tree and gave way to the tears which now streamed from my eyes, the sacrifice that is acceptable to you. . . . I felt that I was still the captive of my sins, and in my misery I kept crying "How long shall I go on saying 'tomorrow, tomorrow'? Why not now? Why not make an end of my ugly sins at this moment?"[22]

Augustine's tears of anguish suddenly led to joy when he took up the Bible and opened it at St Paul's words to the Romans. "I had no wish to read more and no need to do so," Augustine recalled. "For in an instant . . . it was as though the light of confidence flooded into my heart and all the darkness of doubt was dispelled."[23]

Another great weeper of Christianity was Ignatius Loyola, the founder of the Jesuits. One of his ideas was to create a setting for religious conversion, specifically a 30-day retreat which was "a wracking, painful experience as well as an extremely joyful one".[24] Acutely aware of the way in which humans suffered in the world, Ignatius was himself never far from tears. It is said, "his doctors warned him that if he continued to weep so bitterly during Mass, he might lose his sight".[25]

Empathetic tears are similarly shed in the moral stories of eastern faiths. Strikingly, however, such weeping is as often over the perpetrator as the victim of suffering. Reflecting the general Confucian belief that he who turns his back on *jen*, or human-heartedness, hurts himself most, Chinese tales such as this make us pity a woman who beats her child:

> There was a boy who was spanked by his mother every time he did something wrong. Even though it hurt . . . he would not cry. Then, one day, he did something wrong and his mother beat him again. This time, the boy cried.
>
> His mother was surprised and asked: "Why do you cry today when you never cried before?"
>
> "Mother," the boy replied. "In the past when you beat me, it always hurt. But this time, it doesn't hurt any more. I realise it is because you are getting old. That is why I'm crying."[26]

In Buddhism, the tradition of pitying the sinner is particularly strong, as illustrated by several episodes in the *Jataka Stories*, a collection of reincarnation legends surrounding the Buddha's earlier lives. In one pointed tale, a brahman, or religious devotee, prepared for slaughter a goat in contravention of Buddhism's ban on animal sacrifice. At the point of death, the goat both laughed and cried. It laughed because it knew its murder would be the last of 500 lives, each ending with decapitation — a fate which it had had to endure as punishment for sacrificing a goat when it was a brahman some 500 births previously. The goat cried because it knew the brahman would have to suffer the same fate of death and rebirth for his crime.[27]

So crying for someone doing harm to himself or herself is all too appreciable in modern society. Those who witness such self-destructive behaviour as drug abuse or suicide in family members or friends will testify that there is little else one can do but cry. While it may appear futile, weeping at other people's self-harming behaviour could be the best, or most moral, thing to do — for it asserts that human life is valuable. That such crying is awkward and uncomfortable is all the more reason to do it. As Aristotle said, the mark of virtue is "the harder course".[28] It is hard to empathise — to let oneself cry — when one's instinct is to remain aloof from other people's troubles. Or, as the twentieth-century Jewish prophet Abraham Joshua Heschel observed: "Most human beings insulate themselves from suffering to stop themselves from going mad." But to do so "is to lose a sense of urgency and responsibility — a sense that something must be done".[29]

Such is empathy: a sense that "something must be done". It is not a prescriptive virtue. It offers no easy answer to the question of human suffering. But it makes finding an answer a moral imperative.

So described, empathy can be seen as a primitive form of compassion, the virtue we will turn to next. Compassion demands not just tears but a helping hand; and, as such, is a more prescriptive virtue. But why then treat empathy as a virtue in its own right? For this reason if no other: because we have become unmoved by the suffering of others. Witness, for example, the lack of feeling shown towards the estimated 30,000 children dying each day in the developing world through largely preventable diseases like malaria, tuberculosis and HIV.[30] Is it any coincidence, moreover, that such lack of feeling flourishes in a culture that denies the reality of human suffering?

A strain of thought growing ever-more popular in affluent, western societies is that science will ultimately liberate man from ageing, illness, and even death. The thinking goes that suffering is an aberration rather than an integral part of life. And that this view has taken hold is reflected in the fact that natural disasters, like earthquakes or tornadoes, have never been greeted with as much bewilderment as today. Yet why are we surprised that people suffer in the world? Why are we surprised that we grow old and eventually die? We can only be surprised if we lack the sort of empathy shown by the Buddha, or Tolstoy, and forget that death is inevitable, as Utnapishtim said, "both for Gilgamesh and for a fool".

Despite the modern prophets of death-denial, however, there are signs that people have retained some awareness of the reality of suffering, along with a capacity to empathise. One indicator perhaps is the reported upsurge in crying among men, although just how many are crying out of empathy is open to debate. In the US, men are now said to cry 1.4 times a month on average, while research in the UK suggests men there weep at least once a month.[31] Add to this the fact that weeping today tends to be regarded as a strength rather than a weakness in political spheres and there are grounds for arguing that empathy remains at least an ideal, whatever about a reality, in modern society. Indeed, few acts generate as much disgust today as politicians shedding crocodile tears. Movie-stars weeping at award ceremonies with affected gusto come close to matching the offence. We rightly feel aggrieved when we see such phoney tears because they are an affront to empathy. Our disgust mirrors our respect for that most basic of virtues — a virtue from which all others arguably flow.

In Buddhism, there is no argument about it. Empathy is the starting point on the moral journey to enlightenment. It lies at the root of *The First Noble Truth*; namely, "life is suffering". Stemming from the story of *The Four Sights*, the "truth" holds that anyone who looks outside of themselves will see how suffering exists, unavoidably, in the lives of men. From this follows three other claims, first, that suffering is caused by craving; second, that suffering can have an end; and, third, that there is a path which leads to the end of suffering — the way of the Buddha.

Other traditions draw different conclusions from empathetic observations, but the virtue is a common thread throughout. From empathy springs principles of reciprocity, notions (of which we shall read more in the next chapter) to the effect that we should treat others as we wish them to treat us.

So too is empathy necessary for rationalistic moral philosophies, like that, say, of John Rawls. In his influential *A Theory of Justice*, Rawls argued that ideal laws could only be brought about if citizens placed themselves behind a "veil of ignorance" relating to their status in society. Before any moral code could be drafted, people had to empathetically imagine they were born poor rather than rich, disadvantaged rather than privileged, and sick rather than healthy. Empathy lies at the root of continental philosophy too, albeit in other guises. Martin Heidegger called it *angst* (anguish), which he translated specifically as "awareness of death". His thinking was explained thus:

> Anguish may be said accordingly to function as a prelude to a caring for Being; it is that call of conscience [*Gewissen*] which reminds us that the meaning of the world is not simply invented out of our private subjectivity but is given to us by Being itself.[32]

Empathy, in this sense, can be seen as a founding virtue, at the root of human goodness, and essential to moral codes in both religious and secular philosophies. The Buddha, in the story that opened this chapter, may not have helped the old man, the sick man or the dead man's family. But he realised something must be done in the face of human suffering. What that something is we now turn to.

Endnotes

---

[1] Adaptation from various accounts of the tale. See, for example, "The Four Sights" in Ganeri, A. (2001), *Buddhist Stories*, London: Evans, pp. 11–14.

[2] In conventional accounts of the story, the Buddha is portrayed as "saddened and disturbed" by the "four sights". The fact that he tends not to weep openly in renditions of the tale perhaps stems from a prejudice among story-tellers who view crying as a weakness.

[3] Ganeri, A., *op. cit.*, p. 28. The Buddha's final words have elsewhere been translated as: "Decay is inherent in all things: be sure to strive with clarity of mind (for nirvana)." See Keown, D. (1996), *Buddhism*, Oxford University Press, p. 28.

[4] Abu Laylah, M. (1999), *Faith, Reason and Spirit*, Cairo: Al-Falah Foundation dd, p. 52.

[5] Abu Laylah, M., *op. cit.* p. 53.

[6] Dalley, S. (translator) (1991), *Myths from Mesopotamia*, Oxford University Press, pp. 95–101.

[7] Dalley, S., *op. cit.* p. 107.

[8] Cantwell Smith, W. (1989), *Towards A World Theology*. London: Macmillan, p. 7.

[9] Tolstoy, L. as cited in Cantwell Smith, W., *op. cit.* p. 7.

[10] Some scientific research questions whether man is unique in having a conscience. A study at Emory University in Atlanta, Georgia suggests that monkeys have a finely developed sense of fairness. See *The Economist* magazine, 20 September 2003, p. 83. A separate — and unanswered — question is whether animals are capable of death-awareness. The philosopher Arthur Schopenhaur argued that a distinguishing characteristic of man was that "he actually *knows* of death, while the animal only instinctively flees it without

actually knowing of it and therefore without ever really having it in view, which man does all the time".

11 *The Doctrine of the Mean*, 20.

12 Mencius, 4B:6.

13 Adapted from Knappert, J. (1985), *Islamic Legends* (Vol 1), The Netherlands: E.J. Brill, pp. 229-233.

14 Ruthven, M. (2000), *Islam in the World* (second edition). New York: Oxford University Press, p. 181.

15 Knappert, J., *op. cit.* pp. 300-302.

16 Knappert, J., *op. cit.*, p. 302.

17 Bahgat, A. (1997), *Stories of the Prophets*. Cairo: Islamic Home Publishing & Distribution, pp. 371-2.

18 John 11:35.

19 Luke 19:41-42.

20 Hebrews 5:7.

21 Matthew 26: 36-39.

22 Book VIII 12 in Pine-Coffin, R.S., (translator) (1961), *Confessions*, New York: Dorset Press, p. 177.

23 Pine-Coffin, R.S., *op. cit.*, p. 178.

24 Armstrong, K, *op. cit.*, p. 327.

25 Armstrong, K, *op. cit.*, p. 328.

26 Tang, C. (1996), *A Treasury of China's Wisdom*, Beijing: Foreign Languages Press, pp. 89-91.

27 For a full account of this story, see Amore R.C. and Shinn L.D., (1981) *Lustful Maidens and Ascetic Kings*, New York: Oxford University Press, pp. 100–1.

28 Book II (iii) as cited in by Thomson. J.A.K. (translator) (1977), *The Nicomachean Ethics*, Middlesex, England: Penguin, pp. 96–97.

29 Heschel, A.J. quoted in Fashing, D.J. and Dechant D. (2001), *Comparative Religious Ethics: A Narrative Approach*, Massachusetts: Blackwell, p. 189.

30 As estimated by the United Nations Development Programme, 2005.

31 *Sunday Times*, 19 September 2004.

32 Kearney, R. (1994), *Modern Movements in European Philosophy* (second edition), Manchester University Press, p. 36.

2

COMPASSION

There was once a man who was going down from Jerusalem to Jericho when robbers attacked him,
stripped him, and beat him up, leaving him half dead. It
so happened that a priest was going down that road;
but when he saw the man, he walked on by, on the
other side. In the same way a Levite also came along,
went over and looked at the man, and then walked on
by, on the other side. But a Samaritan who was trav-
elling that way came upon the man, and when he saw
him, his heart was filled with pity. He went over to
him, poured oil and wine on his wounds and bandaged
them; then he put the man on his own animal and
took him to an inn, where he took care of him. The
next day he took out two silver coins and gave them
to the innkeeper. "Take care of him," he told the innkeeper, "and when I come back this way, I will pay
you whatever else you spend on him".[1]

Had the world's faiths nothing else in common but a shared belief in empathy there would be much to work on. Followers and non-followers of different faiths would have a basic standard — a standard of humanity — against which to measure their actions. A person of any faith would rightly be exposed to criticism if he or she failed to empathise.

In reality, however, the world's major faiths have more in common than a plea for "something to be done" in the face of human suffering. Each faith offers a similar remedy — a remedy known generically as the Golden Rule. In Christianity it is, "do unto others as you would have them do unto you";[2] in Buddhism, "consider others as yourself";[3] in Judaism "What is hateful to you do not do to your fellow"[4]; in Islam, "none of you truly believes until he wishes for his brother what he wishes for himself".[5]

The Golden Rule informs our desire for justice, fairness and the equal treatment of innocents — of which we shall read more in later chapters. In the first instance, however, the rule provides us with a definition of compassion. To treat others as you would wish them to treat you is the compassionate ideal as embodied in classic morality tales like *The Good Samaritan*.

In the story, the Samaritan — a stranger in the land — does not discriminate against the man whom he encounters even though they are from different countries. Nor does the Samaritan ask what led the man to being beaten up and stripped naked. *Perhaps the man was a bandit who fell out with fellow thieves. Perhaps he was a blasphemer who had been rightly punished for his crimes. Perhaps the man was asking for it.* These thoughts never crossed the mind of the Samaritan. But can the same be said for the Levite, or the priest? Understanding why they did not stop is as important to the morality tale as appreciating why the Samaritan did so.

It is possible that both the Levite and the priest empathised with the beaten man, and maybe even shed a tear as they walked past. The priest could have been inspired by the pitiful sight to give a sermon against robbery. The Levite could have been inspired — like the Buddha — to search for an answer to the question of human suffering in the world. At some point, however, as they saw the man on the side of the road, both the priest and the Levite thought of an excuse not to help.

Their prevarication and ultimate failure to act are all too resonant of social norms today. How many of us even blink when we encounter people in need in our daily lives, let alone stop to help in the manner of a Good Samaritan? We are full of "good excuses" as to why we can't assist others. *I'm too busy. Someone else will do it. I can't make a difference.* Such thoughts constantly run through our minds, perhaps chief among them the latter.

The defeatist notion that we are incapable of affecting change has been particularly dominant in our approach to the Third World. For many years, we tended to blame the ills of Africa on "acts of God" over which we supposedly had no control. Today, we blame them largely on corruption - an undoubted problem in developing countries but surely not an excuse not to help. The fatalist view that we can't alleviate human suffering can be seen as a form of the ancient belief that we are all pawns is some divine chess game, with no control over our own destinies. Ironically, or perhaps not, religion has the potential to fuel such thoughts by suggesting God has "willed" everything that happens in the world, whether it be good or evil.

Different faiths use different means of squaring the circle of human freedom in a God-given world, the Christian theory of "free will" among them. None, however, endorses fatalism as a guide to life even though we may be, in some kind of divine sense, all part of God's "plan".In Judaism, the dilemma is resolved in a Talmudic story about a dialogue between Jewish scholars. In the story, the first scholar suggests that man's duty is — symbolically speaking — to pass the man on the road to Jericho.

> "Suppose," the scholar postulates, "an earthly king was angry with his servant and put him in prison and ordered that he should be given no food or drink, and a man went and gave him food and drink. If the king heard, would he not be angry with him? And you are called 'servants', as it is written, 'For unto me the children of Israel are servants.'"
>
> But the second scholar presents a rival scenario: "Suppose an earthly king was angry with his son, and put him in prison and ordered that no food or drink should be give to him, and someone went and gave him food and drink. If the king heard of it, would he not send him a gift? And we are called 'sons', as it is written, 'Sons are ye to the Lord your God.'"[6]

In the telling of the story, the second view wins out. "The fact that God's judgement has condemned an individual to poverty does not allow us to sit in judgement on that person and to desist from giving help; on the contrary, we are challenged to vigorous ethical response to his or her situation."[7]

Aside from (wrongly) blaming "God's will", what other "good excuses" against helping could the priest or Levite have come up with on the road to Jericho? One was the thought — and it remains a common thought today — that man's duty was merely to avoid causing harm, rather than actually to help someone who had been harmed. This convenient belief can be strengthened by negative formulations of the Golden Rule, which speak only about *not* reciprocating harm rather than reciprocating good.

Certain faiths are more closely associated with the negative rule than the positive one, Confucianism being a notable example. Modesty is a core virtue within the faith and because of this there can be a tendency in Confucian thought towards a minimalist, non-interventionist, ethic. "Doing unto others what you wish done unto you" appears all too presumptuous for some Confucian tastes. An added factor in Confucianism is the influence of Mencius, who believed man to be innately good.[8] Such a positive view of human nature inevitably leads to an ethic which emphasises avoiding harm rather than doing good. (Why, after all, be concerned about doing good if one is good already?) A contrasting opinion can be found in Roman Catholicism, whose doctrine of "original sin" paints a gloomy picture of man's basic instincts. According to orthodox Catholic teaching, as endorsed by St Augustine, people are inherently flawed and can only be saved from a life of sin, not to mention eternal damnation, by conversion to Christianity and the performance of good works. The theory goes that baptism "purges" man of his original sin but doesn't guarantee him Heaven; that comes only if he lives a good life on earth, and in particular avoids mortal sin. Notwithstanding Mencius's influence, however, Confucianism has a place for both negative and positive Golden Rules, translating them respectively as *shu* (altruism) and *chung* (conscientiousness). The former undoubtedly has a special place in Confucian thought, as illustrated by this oft-quoted passage from the *Analects*:

> Confucius was asked by his student Tzu-kung, "Is there one word which can serve as the guiding principle for conduct throughout life?" Confucius replied, "It is the word altruism (*shu*). Do not do to others what you do not want them to do to you."[9]

But does that mean *shu* should be ranked ahead of *chung* ("do unto other what you wish done unto you") in some sort of ethical hierarchy? Confucius was loath to answer in the affirmative. Indeed, having defined *shu* and *chung*, as alternative manifestations of *jen*, the over-arching virtue of human-heartedness, Confucius tended to blend the two together when it came to expanding on their meaning. Another exchange in the *Analects* illustrates the point:

> Chung-kung asked about humanity (*jen*). Confucius said, "When you go abroad, behave to everyone as if you were receiving a great guest. Employ the people as if you were assisting at a great sacrifice. Do not do to others what you do not want them to do to you. Then there will be no complaint against you in the state or in the family."[10]

Elsewhere, "the Master" seemed to elevate "positive" manifestations of *jen* above negative ones. He is reported in the *Analects*, for example, saying:

> "The man of *jen* is one who, desiring to sustain him-
> self, sustains others, and desiring to develop himself,
> develops others. To be able from one's own self to
> draw a parallel for the treatment of others; that may
> be called the way to practise *jen*."[11]

And, in the *Doctrine of the Mean*, Confucius is found to remark:

> There are four things in the Way of the superior man
> . . . To serve my father as I would expect my son to
> serve me . . . To serve my ruler as I would expect my
> ministers to serve me . . . To serve my elder brothers
> as I would expect my younger brothers to serve me. .
> . . To be the first to treat friends as I would expect
> them to treat me. . . . In practising the ordinary vir-
> tues and in the exercise of care in ordinary conversa-
> tion, when there is deficiency, the superior man never
> fails to make further effort, and when there is excess,
> never dares to go to the limit.[12]

The difficulty in maintaining a distinction between "positive"
and "negative" Golden Rules is understandable, given "not
harming someone" can require the performance of certain
acts. To avoid causing a pauper to starve, for example, a
debt-collector may have to cancel the poor person's debt.
Similarly, helping someone out of trouble can require inactivity. A child who steals to feed his family, for instance, may be
helped by not reporting the theft. Or, for a more colourful
example, consider this Palestinian Arab folktale of Mary — a
revered figure in Islam, as in Christianity — as she fled from
persecution with the infant Jesus:

> One night, "Our Lady" came to a sheepfold and hid
> among the ewes which were penned in there. They

didn't stir or utter a sound as she slept, and when she left the next morning she thanked the animals for their protection.

The next night, however, she crept among a herd of goats which, at once, began to bleat. Mary cursed the goats, and straightaway their tails, which up to then were hanging down like those of other animals, lifted and curled upwards.

Since that day, all goats walk with their shameful parts uncovered for all to see.[13]

Compassion sometimes means doing nothing but not always; on this the world's great faiths do agree. Each faith may lend itself towards either a positive or a negative version of the Golden Rule. But no faith adheres solely to a negative one. Indeed, the focus of religious and moral teaching worldwide seems to be as much on the performance of "good works" as on the non-performance of bad ones.

What "good works" are we talking about? Each faith has its favourites. Islam is replete with stories about the value of aiding beggars and of neighbourly affection. In Buddhism, a distinguishing theme is comforting the bereaved over their loss, while Christianity is notable for its focus on visiting the sick and, perhaps uniquely, prisoners.

Such differences can be over-stated, however, and more often than not, the same "good works" are celebrated in different faiths. "Whoever would tend me, he should tend the sick," said the Buddha — using a line that could have come straight from the Bible.[14]

Where faiths do differ is in the scope of their compassion, most notably in respect to animals. A clear dichotomy exists between eastern and western faiths regarding care and consideration towards lesser beasts than man. Those faiths that believe man is reborn as animal, and *vice versa*, in a near-endless cycle of reincarnation, are unsurprisingly less dis-criminatory in their compassion. Where other faiths limit the Golden Rule of reciprocity to the human race, Jainism, Hindu-ism and Buddhism extend it to all living creatures. "Since all beings seek happiness and shun suffering, one should never do anything to another that one would not like to be done to oneself," runs one Buddhist text.[15]

This moral is hammered home in the *Jakata Stories* where characters are celebrated or condemned, depending on the scope of their compassion. One tale describes a king's im-palement for a theft he did not commit. As he lay dying, he became aware of his past lives and realised his grisly fate was punishment, not for the alleged theft, but for impaling an in-sect with an ebony splinter in a former existence.[16]

The Buddha himself provided followers with a positive example of compassion, showing care and consideration to-wards an injured swan as a child. The then Prince Siddhartha wanted to heal the swan while his cousin Devadatta wanted to execute it, having initially shot it down with an arrow. The king settled the dispute in favour of the prince, and future Buddha, when an elderly sage advised: "No one wants to feel pain or die, and it's just the same for animals . . ."[17]

For both Buddhists and Hindus, a guiding principle is *ahimsa*, or respect for the sanctity of life — *all* life. Gandhi, for one, was devoted to this principle, as illustrated by many an episode in his autobiography. Once, some Bengali friends invited him to dinner and served up lamb.

> "To my mind," Gandhi told his hosts, "the life of a
> lamb is no less precious than that of a human being. I
> should be unwilling to take the life of a lamb for the
> sake of the human body. I hold that, the more help-
> less a creature, the more entitled it is to protection
> by man from the cruelty of man."[18]

Gandhi's compassion for all living creatures was taken to extraordinary, and some might say irresponsible, extremes. On
more than one occasion, he refused to allow family members
who had fallen ill to be treated with animal foods, like chicken
broth, eggs or even milk, despite the best advice of local doctors.

> "Rightly or wrongly," he explained, "it is part of my
> religious conviction that man may not eat meat, eggs,
> and the like. There should be a limit even to the
> means of keeping ourselves alive."[19]

Gandhi's may be a minority view in western faiths. Yet they
too discourage cruelty to animals. Islam is perhaps more explicit than Christianity in this regard, with the Qur'an refer-
ring to "all the beasts that roam the earth and all the birds
that fly with wings" as "nations like your own [which will be]
gathered before their Lord [on Judgement Day]".[20]

A textbook on Islamic morals describes a Muslim's duty
thus: "Mercy and kindness should characterise all aspects of
the treatment of animals."[21] The same sentiment is reflected
in a *hadith*, or saying attributed to Muhammad, which runs:

> A man walking along a path felt very thirsty. Reaching a
> well, he descended into it, drank his fill, and came up.
> Then he saw a dog with its tongue hanging out, trying

to lick up mud to quench its thirst. The man said, "This dog is feeling the same thirst that I felt." So he went down into the well again, filled his shoe with water, and gave the dog a drink. So, God thanked him and forgave his sins. The Prophet was asked, "Messenger of God, are we rewarded for kindness towards animals?" He said, "There is a reward for kindness to every living animal or human."[22]

In contrast, Jesus said little about caring for animals, although many Christians believe such caring to be an essential part of the faith. In recent years, PETA, the lobby group for the ethical treatment of animals, ran a campaign on the theme "Jesus was a vegetarian", relying mainly on quotes from the Old Testament about the meat-free Garden of Eden as "God's perfect world". The evidence was fairly flimsy and countered by other references in the Bible to the value of fishing, and Jesus' own practice of meat-eating. But, ultimately, PETA wasn't trying to rewrite history. Rather, it was seeking to question a tendency to limit the scope of Christian compassion to human beings alone.

> Jesus' message is one of love and compassion [ran PETA's campaign literature]. Yet there is nothing loving or compassionate about factory farms and slaughter-houses, where billions of animals live miserable lives and die violent, bloody deaths.[23]

However one defines the Christian position on animal welfare, it should be pointed out that Christianity is not alone in ranking human beings ahead of other life forms in its moral outlook. As one expert in Buddhist ethics points out:

Human beings remain the primary focus of Buddhist teachings and since the basic aim of Buddhism is to guide human beings from the darkness of suffering (*duhkha*) to the light of liberation, this should come as no surprise. In adopting what is in many respects an anthropomorphic position (the view that value belongs to humans alone and nature is to be protected for their sake and no other), the Buddhist view of nature may not be as far removed from the Christian one as is sometimes thought.[24]

Comparing stances on animal welfare raises a more fundamental question about compassion within the world's main faiths: How inclusive should it be? And, in particular, are there people undeserving of compassion? Members of rival faiths, for instance? Or foreigners?

All religions seem to have blind-spots, where one category of individual is singled out — to a greater or lesser degree — for special treatment, or rather ill-treatment, because of race, gender or faith. With Confucianism it is women; Hinduism "untouchables"; Islam apostates, or Muslims who renounce their faith; Catholics Protestants and Protestants Catholics. But is such discrimination inherent to religion? Or is it man-made — a product of human interpretation, or rather misinterpretation, of holy texts?

Debate rages within each faith on these questions. In Hinduism, for example, conservatives claim that each caste has its own moral responsibilities or duties (*dharma*), and that these must be practised distinctly. But reformers, such as Gandhi, argued that all people were subjected to the same universal ethic. Gandhi led by example in this regard, inviting "untouchables" to live with him at his commune home despite the threat of boycotts from other castes.

While some Hindus found a resolution to this dispute that satisfied their beliefs, others did not. Among the latter was Dr B.R. Ambedkar, who believed Hinduism to be hopelessly discriminatory. "To get human treatment, convert yourselves," he told *dalits* (untouchables). "Convert for securing equality. Convert for getting liberty. . . . Why do you remain in that religion which prohibits you from entering a temple . . . from drinking water from a public well? Why do you remain in that religion which insults you at every step?" asked the politician and social activist, who himself converted to Buddhism before his death.[25]

Defining the scope of compassion has proved equally problematic in other faiths. All historically have discriminated against certain groups. All have chosen, at one time or another, to exclude certain people from their application of the Golden Rule. But before we rush to judgement on whether one faith is more or less discriminatory than another we should consider the example set by the wider world.

When have humans ever applied the Golden Rule universally? As the Australian philosopher Peter Singer points out, there has always been a preference in so-called civilised societies for those "of our own kind", be it family, friends, or countrymen. Singer argues that there is an "impartial justification" for approving of parental love, as well as friendship, for, he says, "to suppress these partial affections would destroy something of great value". But, he asks, why should we show more compassion to a neighbour's child, ten yards away from us, than to a starving Bengali child whose name we shall never know, ten thousand miles away? Singer challenges us to come up with a rational answer to the question, and he does so by picturing scenarios like the following:

> [I]magine that on my way to give a lecture, I pass a shallow pond. As I do so, I see a small child fall into it and realise that she is in danger of drowning. I could easily wade in and pull her out, but that would get my shoes and trousers wet and muddy. I would need to go home and change, I'd have to cancel the lecture, and my shoes might never recover. . . . [T]he vast majority of us living in the developed nations of the world have disposable income that we spend on frivolities and luxuries, things of no more importance to us than avoiding getting our shoes and trousers muddy. If we do this when people are in danger of dying of starvation and when there are agencies that can, with reasonable efficiency, turn our modest donations of money into life-saving food and basic medicines, how can we consider ourselves any better than the person who sees the child fall in the pond and walks on?[26]

Western industrialised nations have proven particularly adept at excluding Africa from their application of the Golden Rule. In areas like trade, development aid and security, we never treat Africans in the manner in which we would like them to treat us. As Bono remarked in the run-up to the 2005 G8 Summit:

> Africa makes a fool of our idea of justice; it makes a farce of our idea of equality. It mocks our pieties, it doubts our concern, it questions our commitment. Because there's no way we can look at Africa — a

continent bursting into flames — and if we're honest
conclude that it would ever be allowed to happen
anywhere else. You see, deep down, if we really accepted the Africans were equal to us, we would all do
more to put the fire out.[27]

No faith, nor society, should be hasty to claim a monopoly on
compassion. Each faith may support the Golden Rule but all
have had trouble implementing it universally. That perhaps is
how it must be for the Golden Rule is an ideal, and human
beings — as the priest and Levite showed — are fallible.

Endnotes

[1] Luke 10: 25-37

[2] Luke 6.31

[3] *Dhammapada* 10.1 as quoted in Borg, M. (eds) (1997), *Jesus and Buddha: The Parallel Sayings.* Berkley, California: Ulysses Press, p. 15.

[4] *Shabbat* 31a.

[5] Hadith of al-Bukhari.

[6] Adapted from translation of Babylonian Talmud, *Bava Batra* 10a, as quoted in Solomon, N. (1994), "Judaism" in J. Holm (ed.) *Making Moral Decisions*, London & New York: Continuum, p. 125-6.

[7] Solomon, N., *op. cit.*, p. 126.

[8] Mencius's positive view of human nature has never been universally accepted in Confucianism. Another immediate disciple of Confucius, Hsun Tzu, believed people to be inherently flawed, as will be discussed in the chapter on Loyalty. The difference in opinion, however, did not produce any major schism in Confucian ethics. The relative supporters of both Mencius and Hsun Tzu have come to similar conclusions about how people should ideally be.

[9] *The Analects* 15:23.

[10] *The Analects* 12:2.

[11] *The Analects* 6:28.

[12] *The Doctrine of the Mean* 13.

[13] Bushnaq, I. (1986), *Arab Folktales*. London & New York: Penguin Books, p. 298-9.

[14] Vinaya, Mahavagga 8.26.3 as quoted in Borg, M. *op. cit.*, p. 21.

[15] Keown, D. (1996), *Buddhism: A Very Short Introduction*, Oxford University Press, pp. 95-6.

[16] Garrett Jones, J. (1979), *Tales and Teachings of the Buddha*, London: George Allen & Unwin, p. 41.

[17] Ganeri, A. (2001), *Buddhist Stories*, London: Evans, pp. 9–10.

[18] Gandhi, M.K. (1927), *An Autobiography: or The Story of My Experiments With Truth*. Ahmedabad, India: Navajivan Trust, p. 197.

[19] Gandhi, M.K., *op. cit.* p. 206.

[20] Qur'an 6:38.

[21] Al-Kaysi, M. I. (1986), *Morals and Manners in Islam*. Leicster, England: The Islamic Foundation, p. 193.

[22] Hadith of al-Bukhari as quoted in O'Sullivan, O. (2002), *One God, Three Faiths*. Dublin: Columba, p. 34.

[23] See: www.jesusveg.com.

[24] Keown, D. (2005) *Buddhist Ethics*. Oxford University Press, p.40.

[25] Knott, K. (1998), *Hinduism: A Very Short Introduction*. Oxford University Press, pp. 89-90.

[26] Singer, P. (2004), *One World, The Ethics of Globalization* (second edition). New Haven & London: Yale University Press, pp. 156-7.

[27] Keynote speech to British Labour Party conference, 2004, quoted in *The Irish Times*, 30 September 2004.

3

CHARITY

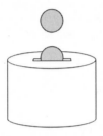

One day Hasan and Hussein, who were still children then, were both ill, and their father asked the Holy Prophet what he could do to relieve their suffering. The Prophet answered that the best therapy would be his fasting. So, Ali, joined by Fatima and their faithful maid-servant Fidha, agreed to fast for three successive days.

Now, as you know, in Islam fasting takes place during the day; at night after dark, people will break their fast with a simple meal, usually some cakes and a drink of milk or fruit juice. So for the first night, Ali went and bought a bag of barley of which Fatima baked five cakes, one for her father, one for her husband, one each for her two sons, and one for herself. Just before sunset a group of very poor people passed who were hungry because they were prisoners-of-war. . . . Ali was moved by pity and gave the cakes to those poor men so that the family had nothing to eat that night.

> The next day, Fatima baked another trayful of five cakes for the night, but before sunset a group of blind beggars [arrived]. . . . Moved by the pitiful appearance of these people . . . the Holy Prophet . . . gave them the five cakes to share among them.
>
> That night again, the holy family fasted, and on the third day, Fatima baked another five cakes for the last night of their fast which they had still not broken. Late that afternoon, however, a group of starving children passed the house, they were orphans who had no house and no family. Full of compassion, Fatima gave away her cakes to the children who did not take long in making them disappear. After this, the holy family spent a third night without breaking their fast.
>
> Soon afterwards God sent down His angel Jibril with the following verses praising the virtue of liberality (Qur'an, 76, 5-10). . . . "The just shall drink of the cup [of Paradisiac beverage] mixed with *kafur*. . . ." Thus Paradise was promised by God to the holy family for their generosity.[1]

Aristotle famously said that the test of virtue was difficulty. He argued that if something was easily done it couldn't be virtuous. The world's great faiths tend to agree, demanding not just that people help each other but that they do so in a particular spirit, namely a spirit of selflessness. "Good works" performed for personal gain are outside of the realm of virtue, they say. Virtue demands both correct action and pure motivation.

Each faith has a unique way of expressing this belief. Confucius, for example, taught "doing for nothing": namely, acting for its own sake and not for material benefit.[2] Establishing a strict division between actions conducted for "profit" and those conducted for "righteousness", he bluntly stated: "The superior man understands righteousness, the small man understands profit . . . If one's acts are motivated by profit, he will have many enemies."[3]

The story above of Islam's holy family illustrates what is called for: that people give without consideration for personal well-being. Ali, Muhammad and Fatima each in turn donated their food to charitable causes despite themselves growing more hungry by the day.

But think for a moment! Were the actions of the holy family completely devoid of self-interest? Their charity may well have been motivated by the promise of heavenly reward — a reward that the angel Jibril (Gabriel) later confirmed would be theirs. They may also have believed that by dispensing charity on their doorstep they could have helped to speed the recovery of Hasan and Hussein in the same way that their fast promised to do so.

Reflect too on what Confucius said: "If one's acts are motivated by profit, he will have many enemies." In the *Analects*, Confucius articulated the corollary of this view: if one's acts are motivated by righteousness, one will have many friends. Moreover, he said, in a passage that echoes somewhat the Christian Beatitudes:

> If one is earnest, one will not be treated with disrespect. If one is liberal, one will win the hearts of all. If one is truthful, one will be trusted. If one is diligent, one will be successful. And if one is generous, one will be able to enjoy the service of others.[4]

How do such spin-off benefits sit with the notion of "doing for nothing"? What is selfless about giving in order to get something in return?

The ambiguity lingers in all religious appeals for selfless action. Are Christians or Muslims who donate to charity entirely free of self-interest, or are they stocking up brownie points for Heaven? Is a Jain monk who sweeps the path before him, to avoid treading on insects, simply trying to safeguard his own safe passage to the next life in a world of reincarnation? Consider too the moral of the *Bhagavad-Gita*, or "Song of God", the epic Hindu myth which centres on a dialogue between the warrior prince Arjuna and the deity Krishna.

Arjuna is depicted at the start of the poem in "hesitation and despondency", facing a battle against kinsmen in order to settle an ancient rivalry. He wonders if it is right to go to war under such circumstances, and turns to his chariot driver, Krishna, for advice. Krishna argues that one can do no wrong so long as one acts without consideration for one's personal welfare. "He who abandons all desires and acts free from longing, without any sense of mineness or egoism — he attains to peace."

Arjuna accepts the point — as every Hindu is supposed to. Crucially, however, the warrior prince refuses to go into battle until he sees "the Divine form" itself, namely God. Arjuna wants final proof of the authority of Krishna's argument. The deity agrees to the request, and so Arjuna "beheld the whole universe, with its manifest divisions gathered together in one, in the body of the God of gods."[5]

The *Gita* teaches that one should act without concern for one's personal welfare. But the story's final turn of events casts doubt on that message. Arjuna says he accepts Krishna's argument about the need to suppress his ego but he won't act on that belief until a miracle, proving God's existence, is performed for his benefit. As he heads into battle, Arjuna's motive is unclear. Is he acting selflessly? Or out of fear, love, or respect, for God, perhaps with the hope or expectation of some divine reward?

The question arises from this and other stories: What do religions mean when they tell us to act selflessly? The answer seems to be that we should act without consideration for *material*, whatever about spiritual or other-worldly, benefits. In the case of charity — as exemplified by Ali, Muhammad and Fatima — that means giving unconditionally and without the expectation of return, except perhaps the spiritual, or emotional, "return" that everyone gets when they feel they have done some good.

One of the material benefits we are told to avoid is public acclaim, and there is no easier way of doing this than to give in secret. Says the Qur'an:

> If ye conceal [acts of charity], and make them reach those [really] in need, that is best for you: it will remove from you some of your [stains of] evil. And Allah is well acquainted with what ye do.[6]

A similar sentiment can be found in the Bible:

> When you give something to a needy person, do not make a big show of it, as the hypocrites do in the houses of worship and on the streets. They do it so that people will praise them . . . But when you help a needy person, do it in such a way that even your closest friend will not know about it.[7]

Eastern faiths teach the same lesson in texts and stories, like the tale *of Sun Shuao and the Twin-headed Snake*. The boy, who would one day become prime minister of the Chinese province of Chu, killed the fearsome snake while out walking one day. When he arrived home, he cried before his mother, saying he had heard that whoever saw a twin-headed snake would not live long.

> "Where is the snake?" his mother asked.
>
> "I killed it, dug a hole and buried it. I did not want other people to see it and go home and die too."
>
> "Good boy!" his mother replied. "You will not die because you have a kind heart. . . . A good deed done in secret will be doubly rewarded."[8]

A variation of the moral can be found in *Aesop's Fables*:

> A wolf had got a bone stuck in his throat, and in the greatest agony ran up and down, beseeching every animal he met to relieve him: at the same time hinting at a very handsome reward to the successful operator. A crane, moved by his entreaties and promises, ventured her long neck down the wolf's throat, and drew out the bone. She then modestly asked for the promised reward. To which the wolf, grinning and showing his teeth, replied with seeming indignation, "Ungrateful creature! To ask for any other reward than that you have put your head into a wolf's jaws and brought it safe out again!"
>
> Those who are charitable only in the hope of a return, must not be surprised if, in their dealings with evil men, they meet with more jeers than thanks.[9]

Each faith lends itself to the same conclusion. The charitable must not only expect no reward but be willing to be taken for a ride. They must risk being labelled gullible or foolish, like Al-Salih, a sultan of Egypt who traced his descent through an ally of the Prophet Muhammad. A popular and just ruler, who shared his wealth with his people and shunned all displays of wealth or power, Al-Salih was sometimes mistaken for a beggar by visiting dignitaries to his homeland. "I am a man at God's gate, robbed of my wits through love of Him," he once said.[10]

Another "charitable fool" in Islamic literature is Hatim al-Tai, who hailed from the twilight years of the Age of Ignorance, the era preceding the Prophet Muhammad. Legend has it that Hatim's mother, when pregnant, was asked in a dream whether she would prefer a generous son called Hatim "or ten like those of other folk, lions in battle, brave lads and strong of limb?" She replied "Hatim" and thus the part-historical, part-mythological figure was born.[11]

As a young boy, Hatim refused to eat his food unless he could share it with other children. If no one could be found he would throw his food away. Later, as he entered adulthood, he was placed in charge of the family herd — only to take a similar approach to his possessions. A group of passing strangers came one day seeking help. Hatim gave them several camels (three in one version of the story, several hundred in another). When his father returned and asked where the camels had gone, Hatim replied:

> "O my father . . . by means of them I have conferred on thee everlasting fame and honour that will cleave to thee like the ring of the ringdove, and men will always bear in mind some verse of poetry in which we are praised. This is thy recompense for the camels."
>
> On hearing these words his father said, "Didst thou with my camels thus?"

"Yes."

"By God, I will never dwell with thee again."[12]

Hatim may have been banished from his tribe but the "simpleton" — as his father called him — was posthumously deified by Muhammad when Hatim's daughter became a prisoner of the Prophet's.

> "My father," she told Muhammad, "was wont to free the captive, and protect those near and dear to him, and entertain the guest, and satisfy the hungry, and console the afflicted, and give food and greeting to all; and never did he turn away any who sought a boon."
>
> To which Muhammad replied: "O maiden, the true believer is such as thou hast described."[13]

Paragons of charity from other faiths suffered similar ridicule and condemnation in wider society, not least Jesus who was spat upon and jeered at as he was led to his Crucifixion. A crown of thorns — the near equivalent to a dunce's hat — was placed on his head. "If you're the son of God," people laughed, "why don't you save yourself?"

Dostoevsky identified this relationship between charity and what society calls foolishness in *The Idiot*. The title refers to Prince Myshkin, a saint-like individual who allows himself be abused and impoverished in the name of virtue. Of the creation, Dostoevsky wrote:

> The main idea of the novel is to depict the positively good man. There is nothing more difficult than this in the world. . . . Of all the good figures in Christian literature, Don Quixote is the most complete. But he is good only because he is at the same time ridiculous.[14]

The type of charity performed by Hatim, Prince Myshkin and Jesus is all the more "ridiculous" today, given the trend towards conditionality in what is now called the charity industry. "You'd be mad to give without looking for something in return"; so we are told in a world where missionary aid is often geared towards saving souls rather than lives, where subsidised food is dumped in developing countries under the guise of humanitarian relief, where B-list celebrities donate time to charity events that "coincidentally" help to resurrect their flagging careers, and where corporations sponsor worthy causes because it is good for their image. Even well-meaning benefactors tend to donate money only if there is some return, such as "structural adjustment" or "good governance", in the case of overseas development aid.

However appealing such practices are, and some are more appealing than others, they do not amount to charity, as understood by the world's major faiths. It may well be that charity is not the right response to certain problems, like poverty in Africa, and that justice — in the form, for instance, of conditional aid — is called for instead. But what we need to be clear of here, in this discussion, is the distinction between charity and other virtues, including justice. Charity is not paying one's due. It is going above and beyond what one owes to society. It is being generous without calculation. It is giving spontaneously, and with no strings attached.

A near-perfect definition of the virtue might be found in the words of a Methodist minister with whom the philosopher Ludwig Wittgenstein stayed in Swansea in 1944. Wittgenstein, who firmly believed that what made an action good was not just its consequence but the spirit in which it was performed, recorded his admiration for the simple dictum which he overheard during his spell in the Welsh guesthouse. The minister's wife had asked Wittgenstein whether he had wanted some tea when her husband interrupted her with the words: "Do not ask; give."[15]

But if we accept this — "Do not ask; give" — as a common definition of charity, a question still remains: *How much?* Islam is perhaps unique among organised faiths in setting a minimum level of charity. Under *zakat*, one of the five pillars of Islam, Muslims donate a specific proportion of their income and capital — traditionally two and a half per cent a year — to less well-off members of the community. Beyond this is *sadaqa*, or voluntary charity, which can be as plentiful as one sees fit.

In Islamic lore, Ali set a high benchmark by not just starving himself to meet the needs of paupers who called to his door but, at one point, giving up his liberty to a Bedouin who asked for help. As legend has it, the prophet's son-in-law had no money to give the Bedouin. So, taking a lead from the Qur'an which declares, with undiscriminating zeal, that "charity is for those in need", Ali offered himself up to be sold as a slave.[16]

Confucianism seems to shun such extravagant displays of charity, suggesting that instead of donating everything to good causes people should only give away excess wealth. A story is recounted whereby a fishmonger gave Confucius a present: the last fish of the day, an unwanted kipper about to be tossed into a bin. Confucius thanked the man and then told his disciples he would offer the fish up to God.

> "This is a fish the man almost threw away," one of his disciple objected. "Why do you want to offer it to God?"

> "If a man understands charity and gives away what
> he does not need," said the master, "he should be
> regarded as a saint. Now I have received a gift from a
> saint, can't I offer it to God?"[17]

What seems like a parable of meanness is, however, the reverse — if, that is, we accept that people need very little. Do
we really need second cars, holiday homes or fashion items?
If not — by Confucian standards — we should give them, or
the monetary equivalent, away.

Christianity puts the same emphasis on ridding oneself of
excess wealth. "Whatever a man has in superabundance is
owed, of natural right, to the poor for their sustenance," said
St Thomas Aquinas. The humanist Peter Singer makes a similar
case, arguing that people have a duty to give "until it hurts".

In conclusion, all virtues — charity included — entail not
just good works but an accompanying spirit of selflessness.
One must be willing to suffer materially to be virtuous, although just how much is open to debate.

Not surprisingly, those with a distorted view of virtue,
like terrorists who claim to be doing God's work, play up the
benefits of what they perceive to be good works. The Al-
Qaeda suicide bombers responsible for the "9/11" attacks in
New York went to their deaths expecting various pleasures
in heaven, from powers to intercede for their relatives on the
day of resurrection to "a home amid rivers of wine and
honey, surrounded by 72 black-eyed virgin wives".[18] Yet any
reading of the Qur'an makes clear that killing on such
grounds not only contradicts Islam's prohibition on suicide
and murder — as will be discussed later— but the faith's de-

mand for selflessness. There is clearly nothing selfless about killing, and dying, for personal reward.

A terrorist might counter with the argument that no one's motives are entirely pure, and indeed, he, or she, might have a point. No less a figure than Gandhi spent a lifetime agonising over the issue, recalling in his autobiography how difficult it was to separate self-interest from actions. Once, he persuaded a legal client to loan money to the proprietor of a vegetarian restaurant in Johannesburg that Gandhi — a vegetarian himself — hoped would flourish. When the business collapsed, Gandhi felt ashamed because, he said:

> "I had disobeyed the cardinal teaching of the *Gita, viz.*, the duty of a man of equipoise to act without desire for the fruit. The error became for me a beacon-light of warning."[19]

Yet, rhetorically, at least, the world's great faiths cling to the notion that one can act selflessly or, in the words of the Buddha, "haste to do good". It is not impossible, they say, to help others spontaneously, or give without any expectation of return. Such giving may seem foolish or even farcical but that doesn't bother the charitable, as this final tale from the Muslim world illustrates:

> Two brothers owned a farm and shared the work and profits equally, even though one was married and had children while the other was a single man.
>
> One night, after harvest, the unmarried brother said to himself: "You know, it isn't really fair. My brother has a wife and family to feed. He should really have a larger share."

So he got up, and crept out of the house and, very quietly, moved six sacks of corn from his own grain store and into his brother's.

Later that night, the married brother woke up, and he said to himself:

"What a lucky man I am. I have a lovely family who care for me, and more than enough food for them. But my poor brother! He has no wife and no children. The least I can do is give him some of my corn."

So he too got up, and went to his grain store, and he too moved six sacks of corn and put them in his brother's store.

The next morning, the two brothers got up and went about their business. Imagine their surprise when they discovered just as many sacks in each store as on the day before!

Neither brother wanted to mention what he had done, for neither wanted to show off his generosity.

But from that year onwards, every harvest time, each brother moved six sacks of grain into the other's store. And every year, the next morning, each one was amazed to find that the number of sacks in his store remained exactly the same.

And neither of them ever found out why.[20]

The moral of the story? Do not ask; give. And keep giving.

Endnotes

[1] Knappert, J. (1985), *Islamic Legends* (Vol. 1), The Netherlands: E.J. Brill, 259–60.

[2] Fung Yu-Lan (1948), *A Short History of Chinese Philosophy*, New York: The Free Press, p. 45.

[3] *The Analects* 4:16, and 4:12.

[4] *The Analects* 17:6.

[5] Radhakrishnan S. and Moore C.A. (eds.) (1957), *A Sourcebook in Indian Philosophy*, New Jersey: Princeton University Press, pp. 101–163.

[6] Qur'an 2:271.

[7] Matthew 6:2–3.

[8] Tang, C. (1996), *A Treasury of China's Wisdom*, Beijing: Foreign Languages Press, p. 86.

[9] Rhys, E. (eds.) (1928), *Aesop's Fables: An Anthology of the Fabulists of All Time*, London: J.M. Dent & Sons, p. 10.

[10] Lyons, M.C. (1995) *The Arabian Epic: Heroic and Oral Story-telling (Vol 1)*, Cambridge University Press, pp. 80–1.

[11] Nicholson R.A. (1969), *A Literary History of the Arabs*, Cambridge University Press, p. 85.

[12] Nicholson R.A., *op. cit.*, p. 86.

[13] Nicholson R.A., *op. cit.*, pp. 86–7.

[14] "Introduction" to Myers, A. (translator) (1992), *The Idiot*, Oxford University Press, p. xv.

[15] Monk, R. (1991), *Ludwig Wittgenstein*, London: Vintage, p. 463.

[16] Knappert, J. (1985), *Islamic Legends (Vol. 2)*, The Netherlands: E.J. Brill, p. 435.

[17] Tang, C., *op. cit.*, p. 59.

[18] *The Economist*, 10 January 2004, p. 18. While some terrorist groups have claimed such prizes await Islamic martyrs, their case is not supported by the Qur'an which makes no explicit reference to the oft-quoted "72 black-eyed virgins". Mention of "chaste women" at 38:52 and "virgin-pure" companions at 56:36 have been cited occasionally. However, recent translations of the Qur'an suggest martyrs for Islam will get "grapes" or "white fruit" rather than a womanly reward, be it virgin or otherwise. See *The Economist*, 29 December 2004.

[19] Gandhi, M.K. (1927), *An Autobiography*, Ahmedabad, India: Navajivan Trust, p. 224.

[20] Adapted from Khattab, H. (1987), *Stories from the Muslim World*, London: Macdonald, pp. 38–9.

4

SELF-DISCIPLINE

Once a samurai came to the master Hakuin and asked, "Master, tell me, is there really such a thing as heaven and hell?"

The master was quiet for some time while gazing at the man. "Who are you?" he asked at last.

"I am a samurai swordsman, and a member of the emperor's personal guard."

"You a samurai!" said Hakuin doubtfully. "What kind of emperor would have you for a guard? You look more like a beggar!"

"What?" the samurai stammered, growing red in the face and reaching for his sword.

"Oho!" said Hakuin. "So you have a sword, do you! I'll bet it's much too dull to cut off my head!"

The samurai could no longer contain himself. He drew his sword and readied to strike the master.

Hakuin responded quickly, "That is hell!"

The samurai, understanding the truth in the master's words and the risk he had taken, sheathed his sword and bowed. "Now," said the master, "That is heaven."[1]

Each faith has one virtue with which it is particularly closely associated. With Christianity it is love, with Islam justice, and with Buddhism self-discipline. Of the three, the final pairing is perhaps the best fit. Whereas the other associations are controversial outside of their respective faiths, the link between self-discipline and Buddhism is universally accepted — so much so that the faith's reputation has suffered.

Many outsiders view Buddhism as an overwhelmingly negative and austere philosophy — a philosophy which, because of its focus on self-restraint, allows, in short, for the least fun. Buddhism's focus on self-restraint is undeniably intense, and is justified by the *Second Noble Truth*, which states that human suffering is caused by acquisitiveness. Greed, hatred and delusion are the "three roots of evil", represented in Buddhist artwork by the cock, pig and snake chasing one another.

How Buddhists are meant to deal with their natural impulses is explained in the penultimate and final noble truths: *The Truth of Cessation* and *The Truth of the Path*, both calling for the sublimation of cravings and the focusing on higher ideals. "People compelled by craving crawl like snared rabbits," said the Buddha. "Those whose compulsions are gone, who are not attached to food, whose sphere is emptiness, singleness, and liberation, are hard to track, like birds in the sky."[2]

Like other faiths based on belief in reincarnation, Buddhism exaggerates the consequences of human faults on the ground that sins cannot be wiped away by confession. Rather, one carries the burden of one's wrongdoing through this life and the next. The lesson is hammered home in countless morality tales where people are condemned for seemingly minor acts of indiscipline. In the *Jakata Stories*, for example, a king who scolds a leper for obstructing his path is reborn as a leper himself.

The ideal within Buddhism is the ascetic monk, someone like Jajali, "who could perform the severest austerities without flinching". As legend has it, he once let a family of Kilinga birds make a nest in his tangled and matted hair — and stood still until the chicks had hatched and flown the nest.[3]

Such bodhisattvas, who try to follow in the footsteps of the Buddha, are compelled not just to take a vow of poverty but one of celibacy. Thus, among trainee monks, "the contemplation of the foul constituents of the body (bile, phlegm, urine, spittle, snot, etc.) was commonly advocated and widely practised."[4] The Buddha led by example in this regard, with one story telling of his encounter with a troupe of erotic dancers. The then Prince Siddhartha, "his heart being estranged from sin, took no pleasure in the spectacle and fell asleep." When he awoke, he saw the women had lain down around him amid "lamps fed with sweet-smelling oil". As legend has it:

> The Bodisat . . . sat cross-legged on the couch, and saw those women with their music truck laid aside and sleeping — some drivelling at the mouth spittle-besprinkled, some grinding their teeth, some snoring, some muttering in their sleep, some gaping, and some with their dress in disorder — plainly revealed as mere horrible occasions of worldly ways.[5]

Meditative self-restraint is particularly associated with Zen, a form of Buddhism which traces its ancestry through a Chinese branch of the faith called Ch'an. Both the story which opened this chapter, and the following tale, are attributed to Zen Buddhism:

Two monks encountered a young woman trying to cross a stream. The elder monk offered to carry her across, and the woman accepted with gratitude.

On the other side, the two monks bade the woman farewell and continued on their journey in silence for a couple of miles.

Then, the younger monk piped up accusingly: "Why did you pick up that young woman? You know monks are not supposed to go near women?"

To which the older monk replied: "You mean you are still carrying her? I left her at the stream."[6]

Non-attachment is recommended not just towards transitory goods, like the pleasures of the flesh. A good bodhisattva is supposed to retreat from all aspects of society — even if it means abandoning friends and family. A salutary tale concerns king Bharata, a sagely ascetic who performed his religious duties beside the Gandaki river until one day he witnessed a pregnant doe fall into the water. There, the doe gave birth and in her misfortune and fright died. The story continues:

Knowing the newborn deer which was floating down the stream to be motherless, Bharata stepped into the stream and rescued the fawn, then started back to his hermitage with the deer under his arm. Although his spiritual duties were numerous, Bharata found time to care for the fawn. Day after day Bharata's affection for the fawn grew as he continued to provide grass and water for its nourishment. . . . Bharata became more and more attached to the young deer as the occasions of fondling or an affectionate kiss multiplied. In the process of showing compassion to the motherless fawn, Bharata finally forgot his spiritual duties and practices and the spiritual advancement that was their goal . . .

When Bharata was near death, he saw the deer sitting by his side exactly like a son lamenting his father's death. As death's veil was spread across Bharata's vision, his mind was fully engrossed with thoughts of the deer and, as a result, he acquired the form of a deer in his new birth! . . . Remembering his past life, Bharata began to lament, "What misfortune I have brought upon myself. I have fallen from the path of the self-realised renouncers. I gave up my wife, family, and kingdom to seek eternal peace in the forest and to become detached from transitory affections and attachments. Instead, I became attached to a deer! Now I have obtained the body of a deer and have fallen far from my devotional practices." Thinking this way, Bharata left his deer family and went off to a forest hermitage to resume his devotional and ascetic practices.[7]

Bharata is not condemned because he showed compassion to the fawn — nothing less is expected of a bodhisattva — but rather because he became obsessed, consumed, by it. A balancing act is thus required whereby one avoids the extremes of both indifference and devotion towards other beings. Moderation is the key, said the Buddha, in this and all endeavours.

The Buddha spoke from experience, having once almost starved himself to death in a failed effort to gain enlightenment. After falling ill through the experiment, he tried gorging himself on life's pleasures but this proved no more productive. In the end, he concluded one should stay away from extremes, and this he taught to his disciples.

The lesson was particularly relevant for monks who had taken to self-flagellation — an understandable lapse in any faith that idealises hardship. Perhaps the most demanding form of Buddhism is Jainism, whose followers are required to ascend through fourteen stages of difficulty, "from the lowest phase of worldliness" to the "final state of bodiless enlightenment". At the tenth such stage, the Jaina practitioner must overcome fourteen separate afflictions, namely: "Hunger, thirst, cold, heat, bites of flies and mosquitoes, travel, learning, lack of intelligence, lack of gain, (rough) sleeping place, injury, ailment, touch of thorny grass and dirt".[8]

One monk who relished in such deprivation was Sona, a contemporary of the Buddha who lacerated his feet so that wherever he walked was "dabbled with blood like a butcher's shambles". The Buddha, however, sat him down and said:

> "Now how say you, Sona? Formerly when you dwelt at home, were you not skilled at playing stringed music on the lute?"
> "Yes Lord."
> "Now how say you, Sona? When your lute strings were overtaut, did your lute then give out a sound, was it fit to play upon?"
> "No, Lord."
> "Now how say you, Sona? When your lute strings were neither overtaut nor overslack, but evenly strung, did your lute then give out a sound, was it fit to play upon?"
> "It was, Lord."
> ". . . [E]xcess of zeal makes one liable to self-exaltation, while lack of zeal makes one liable to sluggishness. . . . Sona, persist in evenness of zeal, be master of your faculties and make that your mark."[9]

In advocating moderation, the Buddha echoed the teachings of another eastern sage, Confucius. In the *Doctrine of the Mean*,

Confucius argued for the middle course as a benchmark in all actions. "The superior man does what is proper to his position and does not want to go beyond this," he said.[10] Instead of drifting from one ambition to the next, people should be "centred" on what else but *jen*, the virtue of human-heartedness. To Confucius, simplicity and restraint were key.

A well-known Chinese story which reinforces the lesson describes how two men once competed in the drawing of a snake. A prize was to go to the artist who finished his drawing first. One of the men, having finished his drawing, saw that his rival was still far behind, and so decided to "improve" his snake by adding feet to it. Thereupon the other man said: "You have lost the competition, for a snake has no feet."[11]

By so calling for balance, Confucius frowned on the self-punishment which was associated with eastern religions. Instead of celebrating poverty, he argued that he would make people rich before trying to teach them — this despite being a great believer in education. Crucially, however, he said, poverty must not be avoided if it means "violation of moral principles". He said: "With coarse rice to eat, with water to drink and with bent arm for a pillow, there is still joy. Wealth and honour obtained through unrighteousness are but floating clouds to me."[12]

Both Confucianism and Buddhism, thus, call for self-discipline. But the virtues they advocate differ in degree. On a spectrum between self-indulgence and self-deprivation, Buddhism tends towards the latter, while Confucianism does so less. The same could be said of Christianity and Islam respectively in a western context. Islam is seen, or at least claims, to be more "balanced" in its approach to key desires, like sexual

appetite and the desire for wealth, than its Abrahamic coun-
terpart. Whereas Christianity tends towards prohibition, Islam advocates assimilation. Or, as one author puts it, with
reference to sexual desire, "Whereas the . . . ideal of Christianity involves a progressive sublimation of the instincts, that
in Islam [and Judaism, which it more closely resembles] is a
symbol of cosmic harmony."[13]

The contrasting approach stems in no small part from the
example of the faiths' founders. According to orthodox Christian teaching, Jesus was a celibate ascetic who condemned
wealth. Muhammad, in contrast, took between five and twelve
wives (there is some debate over the total), and had a successful career in business. Is it any surprise, therefore, that
Islam has a more pragmatic, and perhaps less demanding,
ethic? Muslims prefer to call this ethic "just" — and contrast it
with the otherworldly and "impractical" ethic of rival faiths. As
one Muslim scholar comments, in relation to sexual desire:

> Sex is a strong driving force in the human being which
> demands satisfaction and fulfilment. . . . One way is to
> satisfy one's sexual need freely with whomever is
> available and whenever one pleases, without any re-
> straints of religion, morality, or custom. This is the
> position of the advocates of free sex. . . . The second
> approach is to suppress, and try to annihilate, the
> sexual drive; this approach is advocated by ascetic re-
> ligions and other-worldly philosophies, approaches
> which lead toward monasticism and an escape from
> the world. Such advocacy of suppression of a natural
> appetite, or rather annihilation of its functioning, is
> contrary to Allah's plan and purpose. . . . The third
> approach is to regulate the satisfaction of this urge, al-

lowing it to operate within certain limits, neither sup-
pressing it nor giving it free rein. . . . This is the just
and intermediate position.[14]

Christianity, particularly that form of the faith which celebrates celibacy and monasticism, is regarded as somewhat
"other-worldly" by Islam, and Jesus as something of an eccentric. One Muslim tale describes how Jesus took shelter in a
tent during a violent storm of heavy rain and wind. When he
discovered there were women inside, he fled as fast as he
could and "being a confirmed bachelor" spent the night instead crouched beside a lion in a nearby cave.[15]

Islam also claims to have a more balanced approach to
wealth than Christianity, counselling against greed and exploitation without demonising the desire for material self-
advancement. Commerce is regarded as an integral part of
Islamic life, and several passages of the Qur'an detail rules of
fair trading. Exploitation, including the earning of interest off
the borrowings of fellow Muslims, may be banned. But the
accumulation of riches itself is not. This stems in part from a
recognition of the dehumanising effects of poverty.

Muslims are reminded in the Qur'an that their ancestors
were once driven to killing their children to spare them the
certainty of starvation. One scholar of Arab literature remarks:
"Perhaps the most touching lines in [pre-Islamic] Arabian poetry are those in which a father struggling with poverty wishes
that his daughter may die before him and thus be saved from
the hard mercies of her relatives."[16] A poem from the era, The
Poor Man's Daughter, opens one of its verses with the words:
"She wishes me to live, but I must wish her dead. . . ."[17]

The Qur'an thus advises Muslims to lift themselves out of poverty. But it warns against turning that "just" desire into greed. Muhammad himself lived a very simple life, shunning the accumulation of luxuries or grand displays of wealth. Among other things, he was perhaps the first great prophet to identify the obscenity of lavish weddings. It is recalled:

> In those days, before the spread of Islam, many Arabs gave feasts when their daughters were married. A large number of guests came to the wedding feasts, and the eating and merry-making often went on all night. Rich and costly presents were also given to the newly married couple. But the Prophet (may peace be upon him) was a man of simple tastes. He thought it was wrong to spend money on feasts when many people were too poor to buy bread. So the marriage of Fatima and Ali took place quietly in Medina. The Prophet gave his daughter simple and useful presents. Instead of gold and jewels, he gave Fatima dishes for her house and sheets for her bed.[18]

Like Muhammad, Jesus condemned greed but his answer to the vice was more radical. "Sell all your belongings and give the money to the poor. I tell you not to worry about the food you need to stay alive or about the clothes you need for your body. Life is much more important than food, and the body much more important than clothes," Jesus told his disciples.[19]

In Matthew's Gospel, Christ famously encountered a wealthy young man who asked, "What good thing must I do to receive eternal life?" Jesus answered:

"If you want to be perfect, go and sell all you have and give the money to the poor, and you will have riches in heaven; then come and follow me."

When the young man heard this, he went away sad, because he was very rich.

Jesus then said to his disciples, "I assure you: it will be very hard for rich people to enter the Kingdom of heaven. I repeat: it is much harder for a rich person to enter the Kingdom of God than for a camel to go through the eye of a needle."[20]

Jesus further promised that "everyone who has left houses or brothers or sisters or father or mother or children or fields for my sake, will receive a hundred times more and will be given eternal life". Urging his disciples to lead by example, he said, "Don't take anything on your journey except a stick — no bread, no beggar's bag, no money in your pockets. Wear sandals, but don't carry an extra shirt."[21]

Within Islam, such asceticism is viewed as somewhat extreme. Jesus' own vow of poverty, like his vow of celibacy, is portrayed in Muslim stories as an eccentric, if not comical, commitment. One such tale runs:

Jesus owned nothing but a comb and a cup. He once saw a man combing his beard with his fingers, so Jesus threw away the comb. He saw another drinking from a river with his hands cupped, so Jesus threw away the cup.[22]

But how extreme is Jesus' plea for asceticism? Some Christians believe the "eye of the needle" alluded to in the Gospel is not a metaphor but an actual gate in Jerusalem through which traders passed. As legend has it, a camel could only enter the gate unencumbered and crawling on its knees. If this is true (and it is a big "if" as there is little historic evidence of the gate's existence) Jesus' parable takes on a new meaning: A rich man is capable of entering heaven but only if he first disposes of his worldly goods and prostrates himself before God.

A further argument against extreme asceticism in Christianity is that Jesus never meant all followers to meet the same exacting standards of devotion as his disciples. The argument justifies the differing demands made of clergy and laity in Christian churches. The case for limited asceticism is further supported by references in the Old Testament for people to "be fruitful and increase in number" (Genesis 1:28) (something which, if pursued, would be incompatible with celibacy), and to "show restraint" when trying to get rich (Proverbs 23:4–5). It is telling, however, that Christianity contains no parables in which Jesus warns against over-zealous asceticism. This contrasts with Islam, where Jesus (the Muslim prophet) can be found rebuking converts who weep and tear at their clothes. "What sins have your clothes committed? Turn instead to your hearts and reprove them," the prophet said. Another tale from Islam runs:

> Jesus met a man and asked him, "What are you doing?"
> "I am devoting myself to God," the man replied.
> Jesus asked, "Who is caring for you?"
> "My brother," replied the man.
> Jesus said, "Your brother is more devoted to God than you are."[23]

To some readers, many of the above teachings will seem extreme, and many of the ascetic practices advocated in those teachings unattractive. But does that mean we should dismiss what the world's faiths have to say about self-discipline?

Arguably, we have never been so free in the West; we are free to engage in any number of sexual pleasures, consume no end of alcohol and drugs, make all the money we can and then drown in a sea of luxuries. Perhaps too we have never been so unwilling to listen to religious authorities — with good reason, in some instances, given their recent record of hypocrisy over such matters as sexual morality. But by turning our back on religious instruction, along with its instructors, we perhaps punish ourselves most. One thing is for certain: as religious leaders no longer have the power to discipline us over matters of "personal morality" we must police ourselves. With freedom comes responsibility; this applies as much in the private as in the public sphere. If we want to live ethically we cannot merely be slaves to our passions.

A final thought on self-discipline. It is, as we have seen, an antidote, not just to one vice but to many. We have spoken much about greed and lust, and later we shall read how self-discipline — encapsulated in the virtue of mercy — conquers anger. But before we turn to the next virtue, a final vice of indiscipline deserves mention, if only because it is so pervasive in society today, and that is gossip. The vice should not be confused with slander, for whereas the latter involves the telling of malicious falsehoods about others, gossip is the practice of engaging in idle, unconstrained or reckless speech. It is, in short, a folly but a folly with moral consequences. The lesson is hammered home in the *Jakata Stories* in which we read of a tortoise who struck up a friendship with some wild geese.

One day they said to him: "Master tortoise, we two live on Himalaya, on the slope of Bright Peak, a lovely spot, in a golden cave. Do you come thither along with us?"

"Why friends, how could I get there?"

"We will seize hold of you and go along. If only you can keep your mouth shut, there's nothing you can't do."

"Oh, I'll keep it shut all right," said the tortoise. "Take me up, and off we go!"

"Good!" said they, and took a stick and made the tortoise grip it with his teeth. Then they two, seizing hold of each end of the stick, mounted up into the air.

As they flew along, some village boys saw him being carried by the wild geese and shouted: "Look! Look! A tortoise carried on a stick by two wild geese!"

Then the tortoise, longing to reply: "What is it to you where my friends are taking me, you rascally rogues?" — just when, thanks to the rapid flight of the wild geese, they were right over the Raja's palace at Benares — opened his mouth, let go the stick, fell into the open court of the palace and was split in two.

As the story goes, the sudden crash silenced the Raja, a man known for "boundless babbling". The bodhisattva then spoke:

> "O sure the shellback slew himself,
> Striving his thoughts to tell.
> Safe was he while he grasped the stick,
> But when he spoke, he fell.

> "O best of energetic men,
> Let words be wise and few!
> Thou seest how to chattering
> This shellback's death was due."[24]

Silence, in the form of meditation, is, of course, a core dimension of Buddhist practice. By sitting still in quiet contemplation, the Buddhist develops feelings of calmness and detachment which he or she takes into ordinary life. Buddhism, however, is not alone in celebrating the virtue of silence. "The man who is simple and slow to speak is near to humanity," said Confucius.[25] "Piety is nine-tenths silence and one-tenth fleeing from people," said Jesus, according to Islamic scripture.[26] "When one comes to think of it," said Gandhi, "one cannot help feeling that nearly half the misery of the world would disappear if we, fretting mortals, knew the virtue of silence."[27]

On few other matters are the world's great faiths in such concordance. In unison, they declare — hailing the virtue of self-discipline — that there is a time to speak and a time to shut up. On which note . . .

Endnotes

[1] Davy Pearmain, E. (1998), *Doorways to the Soul*, Cleveland, Ohio: The Pilgrim Press, p. 27.

[2] *Dhammapada* 7:3-4 and 24:9 as quoted in Borg, M. (eds) (1997), *Jesus and Buddha: The Parallel Sayings*, Berkeley, California: Ulysses Press, p. 43 and 89.

[3] Amore R.C. and Shinn L.D., (1981), *Lustful Maidens and Ascetic Kings, Buddhist and Hindu Stories of Life*, New York: Oxford University Press, pp. 148–50.

[4] Garrett Jones J. (1979), *Tales and Teachings of the Buddha: The Jakata Stories in Relation to the Pali Canon*, London: George Allen & Unwin, p. 76.

[5] Rhys-Davids, C.A.F. (1998), *Buddhist Birth-Stories*, New Delhi: Srishti Publishers and Distributors, p. 171.

[6] For another version of this story see: Fashing, D.J. and Dechant D. (2001), *Comparative Religious Ethics: A Narrative Approach*, Massachusetts: Blackwell Publishing, p. 151.

7 Amore R.C. and Shinn L.D., *op. cit.*, pp. 174–6.

8 Chapple, C.K. (2001), 'Pushing the Boundaries of Personal Ethics: The Practice of Jaina Vows', in J. Runzo and N.M. Martin (eds.), *Ethics in the World Religions*, Oxford: Oneworld, p. 204.

9 Woodward, F.L. (1925), *Buddhist Stories*, Madras, India: Theosophical Publishing House, pp. 112–116.

10 The Doctrine of the Mean 14, as quoted in Wing-Tsit Chan (1963), *A Source Book in Chinese Philosophy*, New Jersey: Princeton University Press, p. 101.

11 Fung Yu-Lan (1948), *A Short history of Chinese Philosophy*, New York: The Free Press, p. 100.

12 *The Analects* 7:15.

13 Ruthven, M. (2000), *Islam in the World* (second edition), New York: Oxford University Press, p. 155.

14 Al-Qaradawi Y. (1994), *The Lawful and the Prohibited in Islam*, Indiana: American Trust Publications, pp. 148–9.

15 Assfy, Z.H. (1977), *Islam and Christianity*, York, England: William Sessions Ltd, p. 56.

16 Nicholson R.A. (1969), *A Literary History of the Arabs*, Cambridge University Press, p. 91.

17 Nicholson R.A., *op. cit.*, pp. 91–2.

18 Whyte, R. (1966), *Ten Stories from Islam*, Lahore: Pakistan Branch, Oxford University Press, p. 47.

19 Luke 12:22–34.

20 Matthew 19:16–28.

21 Mark: 6:8–9.

22 Khalidi, T. (2001), *The Muslim Jesus: Sayings and Stories in Islamic Literature*, Cambridge, Massachusetts: Harvard University Press, p. 176.

23 Khalidi, T., *op. cit.*, p. 41 and p. 102

24 Woodward, F.L., *op. cit.*, pp. 107–11.

25 *The Analects* 13:27.

26 Khalidi, T., *op. cit.*, p. 170.

27 *Harijan*, 24 September 1938.

5

LOYALTY

Bilal was a Muslim and slave whose master, Umaya, was one of the most important men among the pagans of Mecca. Umaya was a harsh man who would not allow his slaves to follow any religion other than his own, which was the worship of idols. He decided to force Bilal to give up Islam.

Every day at noon, he had Bilal taken out of the city and made him lie on the scorching desert sand under the burning sun. Then Umaya placed a huge stone on top of his chest.

"You'll stay like that," he said to Bilal, "until you either die or renounce your religion."

But Bilal could not deny his faith.

The sun burned down, and the vultures wheeled overhead. Bilal's mouth was dry and the pain in his chest made it almost impossible for him to breathe. Nonetheless, he held firm. Raising a single finger in the air, he whispered with what seemed like his last breath: "One God, one God."[1]

It will not come as a surprise to hear that the world's major religions demand loyalty. But loyalty to what, or whom? To God or Allah? To a church or a preacher? To family, friends, or the state? The issue is not as straightforward as it may seem, for practising a religion may involve loyalty to a combination of the above. Take Confucianism, for example. Two fundamental virtues in the faith are filial loyalty, and loyalty to the state. It is unclear, however, which should take precedence if and when they clash.

Filial loyalty is described by Confucius as "the root of a man's character", and the bedrock of a civilised society. "Never disobey," the Master said. "When parents are alive, serve them according to the rules of propriety. When they die, bury them according to the rules of propriety and sacrifice to them according to the rules of propriety."[2] And again, "In serving his parents, a son may gently remonstrate with them. When he sees that they are not inclined to him, he should resume an attitude of reverence and not abandon his effort to serve them. He may feel worried, but does not complain."[3]

Stories of filial devotion abound in Confucian literature. One anecdote runs:

> A dutiful boy, worried that his parents would be bitten by mosquitoes, slept naked without covers to encourage the mosquitoes to feed on him, rather than on his parents.[4]

The social benefits of such loyalty are outlined in *The Great Learning*, which states: "When the individual families have become humane, then the whole country will be aroused toward humanity. When the individual families have become compliant, then the whole country will be aroused toward compliance."[5]

Mencius put it more bluntly, saying most of the world's problems would disappear if only children listened to their parents.

As for loyalty to the state, or *li* in Confucianism, the virtue is celebrated as a necessary component of the Heavenly Way — necessary because, left to their own devices, people will inevitably drift towards anarchy. Or so says an influential branch of Confucianism, headed by Hsun Tzu (c 310–237 BCE). If humans were intrinsically good, that is "upright, reasonable and orderly . . . what need would there be for sage-kings and *li*?" he asked. Were all regulative rules removed, and respect for *li* gone "the strong would injure the weak and rob them, and many would do violence to the few and shout them down. The whole world would be in violence and disorder."[6] Hence, Hsun Tzu, along with Confucius, encouraged citizens to serve in public office, and pledge loyalty to the state. "A man who has energy to spare after studying should serve his state. A man who has energy to spare after serving the state should study," runs one Confucian maxim.[7]

Other faiths have mixed views on such loyalties. In Buddhism and Hinduism, excessive loyalty to either parents or friends is seen as a form of weakness, or as an obstacle on the path to enlightenment. Gandhi believed "all exclusive intimacies are to be avoided. . . . He who would be friends with God must remain alone, or make the whole world his friend."[8] Surprisingly, perhaps, Gandhi was enthusiastic about loyalty to the state. "A willing and respectful obedience to the state laws" was a prerequisite for a *Satyagrahi*, or socially concerned religious devotee. As Gandhi put it:

> A *Satyagrahi* obeys the laws of society intelligently and of his own free will, because he considers it to be his

sacred duty to do so. It is only when a person has thus obeyed the laws of society scrupulously that he is in a position to judge as to which particular rules are good and just and which are unjust and iniquitous. Only then does the right accrue to him of the civil disobedience of certain laws in well-defined circumstances.[9]

Islam takes the reverse position, celebrating loyalty to friends and family, and doubting the value of loyalty to the state. As the religious scholar Malise Ruthven points out, Islamic *Shari'a*, or religious, law recognises "no corporate entities (like the church or state) which could be treated as persons in law". A negative consequence of this "has been the lack of legitimacy accorded the public interest in the form of city, state, or any other institution standing between the individual and God."[10] Filial loyalty, on the other hand, is seen as a core virtue in Islam, and disobeying one's parents, particularly one's mother, a grievous sin. It is recalled:

> Once a man came to the Prophet (peace be upon him) and asked, "Who is most deserving of my good companionship?" "Your mother," replied the Prophet. "Who next?" the man asked. "Your mother," replied the Prophet. "Who next?" he asked. "Your mother," replied the Prophet. "Who next?" asked the man. "Your father," replied the Prophet.[11]

Friendship is similarly acclaimed in Islam. "A friend has the right to have the following three things forgiven," says one Muslim scholar, "(a) A transgression in the time of anger; (b) A transgression caused by too much fondness of you, and (c) An unintentional mistake."[12] As one Arab proverb, recommends: "If I should find my friend in the wrong, I reproach him secretly; but in the presence of company I praise him."[13]

Christianity, likewise, allows for a combination of loyalties. The importance of filial devotion is highlighted in both Old and New Testaments. The fifth of the Ten Commandments given to Moses at Mount Sinai was "honour thy father and mother".[14] Jesus subsequently translated this as: "Whoever curses his father or his mother is to be put to death."[15] As for loyalty to the state, Christianity is not blind to its value. Jesus himself implicitly accepted the authority of the Roman Empire when he faced his execution without questioning the legitimacy of the sentence under Roman law. "Pay the Emperor what belongs to the Emperor, and pay God what belongs to God," Jesus famously told his disciples, suggesting Christians can be loyal to both church and state without conflict.[16]

There is, of course, one form of loyalty that is particularly associated with religions, namely loyalty to belief. This kind of loyalty we call faith. At first glance, faith may not seem like a form of loyalty at all. One might argue it is an accident of birth rather than a chosen disposition. Yet the same can be said of loyalty to one's family. Faith resembles other loyalties in that it demands steadfastness in the face of adversity. Just as the faults of our parents challenge our filial devotion so too do the troubles of the world challenge our faith, be it faith in God, or in some other ideal. And, as with other forms of loyalty, faith has its means of display, religious worship and prayer among them.

So understood, faith should not be confused with loyalty to a religious institution, although the lines between the two have traditionally been blurred. Indeed, religious leaders have sometimes argued that loyalty to the institution is the same as faith, or loyalty to belief, in God. For part of the last century, the Catholic Church promoted a catechism that answered the question "Who is a Christian?" with the reply: "One who obeys the Pope and the pastor appointed by him."[17] But, in practice, faith and loyalty to an institution like the Catholic Church can be in competition. Sometimes, Catholics give faith priority — when, for instance, they disobey or disagree with the teachings of the Vatican on the basis of their own understanding of what is right. At other times, they give loyalty to the Church priority, when, for instance, they defend actions it has committed that they know to be wrong. The Church has in recent years admitted that tensions exist between, on the one hand, loyalty to the institution and, on the other, faith in the teachings of Christ. Notwithstanding its claims of papal infallibility, it has furthermore suggested that faith should take ultimate priority, condemning its own practice of putting institutional loyalty first in handling, for example, recent clerical sexual abuse scandals.

Another characteristic of faith is that it is not strictly rational. By being loyal to a particular belief system, the faithful ignore evidence suggesting that this belief system may be incorrect. The classic Christian parable of faith is that of *Doubting Thomas*. It is recalled that Thomas alone among the twelve disciples refused to believe Jesus had risen from the dead.

> The other disciples told him, "We have seen the Lord." But he said to them, "Unless I see in his hands the print of the nails, and place my finger in the mark of the nails, and place my hand in his side, I will not believe."
>
> Eight days later, his disciples were again in the house, and Thomas was with him. The doors were shut, but Jesus came and stood among them, and said, "Peace be with you."

> Then he said to Thomas, "Put your finger here, and see my hands; and put out your hand, and place it in my side; do not be faithless, but believing."
>
> Thomas answered him, "My Lord and my God!"
>
> Jesus said to him, "Have you believed because you have seen me? Blessed are those who have not seen and yet believe."[18]

Faith, thus, should be seen as a special type of loyalty. It is, in a sense, seeing what we want to see, rather than what is. As such, it is regarded by many secularists — particularly those of a rationalist bent — as a vice. But, before addressing such criticism, consider how the world's religions balance faith with other loyalties. In each religion, faith is presented as a special form of loyalty — and one which generally supersedes all others. Muslims are reminded of the primacy of faith in their declaration — made many times a day — that "there is no god but God and Muhammad is the messenger of God". Bilal, the historical character of whom we read at the opening of this chapter, provides inspiration to many followers of Islam, particularly in the United States where the Abyssinian slave became a folk-hero of the black Muslim movement. As the story goes, Bilal was rescued from certain death by Abu Bakr, a friend of Muhammad's who had taught Bilal about Islam. The freed slave was later rewarded for his loyalty to the Prophet with the honour of calling Muslims to worship for the first time ever from the roof of the Ka'ba.

It was no small act of defiance for Bilal to follow Muhammad so. At that time, Muslims had a stark choice: Be loyal to one's family or be loyal to Allah. Indeed, Islam traces its roots to a decision by members of the Quraish tribe from which Muhammad sprung to exchange a familial loyalty for a religious one. The Prophet's earliest followers helped him to establish his own community, or *umma*, by raiding the caravans of their (non-Muslim) kinsmen — a radical departure from Bedouin custom. For Abu Bakr, loyalty to Islam meant going so far as facing down his own son, Abdur Rahman, in the battle of Badr. Abdur Rahman converted to Islam after the war in which the Muslims and pagans were effectively fighting by different rules, as this exchange between father and son illustrates:

> Abdur Rahman looked at Abu Bakr and said, "Father, when you and I fought on opposite sides at the battle of Badr, you came within reach of my sword many times, but I did not kill you because you were my father!"
>
> Abu Bakr replied, "My son, if you had come within reach of my sword at the battle of Badr, I would have killed you! You were an enemy of Islam then, and I would never let even my love for you come between me and Islam."[19]

The idea of a borderless community, in which people are bound together by religious loyalty, was alien to a culture that valued family bonds above all else. Today, the notion of *umma* remains perplexing when convention decrees — in the democratic world, at least — that one's principal loyalty should be to the state. Loyalty to *umma* explains why Muslims in the West feel particularly aggrieved at the suffering of their brethren in Palestine, and elsewhere. This notional loyalty between Muslims, however, should not be confused with loyalty to a spiritual leader or church. *Umma* is not an institution. It has no spokesperson. It is merely an idea — which forms part of Islamic belief — to the effect that Muslims are united in their worship of Allah. It is, in short, a notion of collective faith.

Loyalty to *umma*, therefore, should not be confused with *jihadism*, or the cult-like fanaticism behind such groups as Al-Qaeda. Muslim fanatics claim to be following in the footsteps of Abu Bakr and other holy warriors by turning their backs on — or turning against — their families and their communities. In reality, however, they merely create new bonds of earthly loyalty, be it to an organisation, a spiritual leader, or, worse still, a terrorist "cell". Members of the fundamentalist Muslim Brotherhood, for example, are grouped into "families and battalions", while "young Palestinians who today volunteer for suicide missions are organised into 'friendship packs' who may act as family substitutes, while holding them to their decision."[20] By devoting themselves to fellow extremists above all else, Muslim fanatics only go to prove their disloyalty to God, and Islam.

But what of other religions? Christianity may not have its equivalent of *umma*. Yet Jesus was unequivocal, notwithstanding what he said about filial loyalty, that family bonds must take second place to faith. "Whoever loves his father or mother more than me is not fit to be my disciple," he said. "Whoever loves his son or daughter more than me is not fit to be my disciple."[21]

Significantly, however, these words were spoken to the Twelve Apostles rather than to the crowds who went to hear Jesus speak. To this day, many Christians believe the Apostles — and their latter-day descendants, the clergy — must obey a different, and more exacting, ethic than other followers of Christ. It is important to note, moreover, that the theme of choosing religion over family is not as pronounced in Christian literature, if it is there at all. The

contrast with Islam can be seen in the telling of the story of
the great flood. In the Bible, Noah escaped with his wife and
sons, who would become "the ancestors of all the people on
earth".[22] But in the Qur'an, one of the sons gets left behind
and is drowned, leaving Noah somewhat dismayed. It turns
out the son was secretly a disbeliever who feigned faith in
public, and this fact was conveyed to Noah by Allah. According to one Islamic scholar:

> Almighty Allah wanted to tell his noble prophet that his
> son was not of his people because he did not believe in
> Allah. Blood is not the true bond between people.[23]

What Islam and Christianity do have in common is a culture
of martyrdom. Neither religion is short of historical examples
of followers choosing to die rather than renouncing their
faith. Muhammad, in fact, was admiring of the loyalty which
Christians showed to their beliefs in the face of persecution
by fanatical Jews in the sixth century. When Muslims were in
turn being persecuted, the Prophet "consoled and encouraged his followers by the example of the Christians at Najran,
who suffered 'for no other reason but that they believed in
the mighty, the glorious God'."[24]

Judaism, likewise, celebrates faith-inspired martyrdom, as
encapsulated in figures like Rabbi Akiba ben Joseph (50–135
CE), who was arrested by the Romans, and tortured to
death. It is recalled:

> When Hadrian issued the decree imposing the
> death penalty on anyone who devoted himself to its
> study, Rabbi Akiba gathered his disciples wherever he

could so that their studies could continue. He was asked: "Are you not afraid of the government?"

He replied with a fable: "A fox went to a river and saw the fish scurrying around in great fear. The fox said to them, 'What do you fear and from whom are you fleeing?' The fish replied, 'We flee the nets which men have spread before us.' The fox then said, 'It would be better if you came out on dry land and we would live together just as my forefathers once lived together with your forefathers.' But the fish answered, 'Are you he who is reputed to be the wisest of animals? You are not the wisest but the most foolish. If we are afraid of being caught here in the water, where is the place of our life . . . how much more should we be afraid on dry land where we would die?'"

Rabbi Akiba finished his fable by saying: "The same is true of the honesty of learning. If we are in danger of being caught when we are engaged in the study of Torah, how much greater would be the danger if we should cease to devote ourselves to it?"[25]

In eastern religions, faith tends to be celebrated through deities rather than martyrs. A classic example is Yudhishthira who, at the end of the Hindu epic of the *Mahabharata*, is alone in the world but for a stray dog. Having passed every test of virtue thrown at him, Yudhishthira is greeted by the God Indra who promises to escort him to heaven. Yudhishthira won't depart, however, unless he can take the dog with him — a request that does not go down well with Indra, as dogs are considered pollutants in traditional Indian society. The narrative continues:

> "O King! [says Indra.] You have won immortality and a status equal to mine; all the felicities of Heaven

are yours today. Do cast off this dog. In this there will be no cruelty."

Yudhisthira remained unswayed. They had reached the end of the world. He saw in the helpless gaze of the dog, trembling in the stark, desolate surroundings, an appeal not to be abandoned. Filled with compassion [*anukrosha*], Yudhishthira was not able to disregard this silent cry for the sake of his own happiness. Dismayed by this unexpected obstacle to his mission, Indra lost his temper and railed:

"Not only is this concern for a dog not required of you as a paragon of justice, but it seems that you, who have been able to renounced everything — the love of kingdom, the love of a wife and brothers — have morally stumbled at this last moment and become ensnared and blinded by the irrational love [*moha*] for a dog!"

Refusing to be shamed, Yudhisthira retorted,

"O Indra, I think the sin of abandoning one who is loyal [*bhaka*] is greater than many other sins put together. I cannot leave the dog behind."

[It was then] the dog revealed himself as *dharma* in disguise and explained the entire incident as a final test of moral worth — a test that Yudhisthira passed yet again, with flying colours . . .[26]

The lesson is the same across all faiths: People must be steadfast in their convictions, even if it hurts. As the *Bhagavad-Gita* declares: "Better is one's own law [*dharma*], though imperfectly, carried out than the law of another carried out perfectly. Better is death in the fulfilment of one's own law, for to follow another's law is perilous."[27]

Secularists might concede some admiration for the spirited faith, or *loyalty to belief*, of Bilal, Rabbi Akiba and

Yudhishthira. However, such loyalty tends to be perceived in the secular world as at best misplaced, and at worst down-right dangerous.

That heinous crimes have been committed in the name of faith is undeniable. But is that alone a reason to condemn the virtue? In criticising faith, secularists — or more particularly rationalists — tend to ignore two facts. The first is that hei-nous crimes have been committed historically in the name of other loyalties, such as familial loyalty, loyalty to the state, and loyalty to what the philosopher John Gray describes as "Enlightenment ideals of progress". Gray notes:

> The role of humanist thought in shaping the past cen-tury's worst regimes is easily demonstrable, but it is passed over, or denied, by those who harp on about the crimes of religion. Yet the mass murders of the twentieth century were not perpetrated by some lat-ter-day version of the Spanish Inquisition. They were carried out by atheist regimes in the service of Enlightenment ideals of progress. Stalin and Mao were not believers in original sin. Even Hitler, who despised Enlightenment values of equality and freedom, shared the Enlightenment faith that a new world could be created by human will.[28]

A puzzling aspect of secular criticism of faith is that it tends to see both logic and merit in all forms of loyalty but loyalty to religious belief. The philosopher and outspoken critic of religion Peter Singer, for instance, defends familial loyalty on the grounds that it encourages loving relationships in society. He rightly points out that any attempt to eradicate parental favouritism for their children "would have high costs and would require constant supervision or coercion. . . . If we were to engage in such a campaign, we may well bring about guilt and anxiety in parents who want to do things for their children that society now regards as wrong. Such guilt will itself be a source of much unhappiness."[29] Yet, surprisingly, Singer ignores the fact that the same argument can be made in defence of faith, or loyalty to a particular belief system.

For religious believers, faith provides the impetus for all sorts of good works, including loving and caring for family, friends, and the broader populace. Any attempt to eradicate faith would have a high cost. It would also require constant supervision or coercion and would be unlikely, ultimately, to prove successful; not even Stalin's communist pogroms managed to eradicate loyalty to religious belief in twentieth-century Russia. Morever, campaigning against faith would undoubtedly bring about guilt, anxiety and unhappiness in those who wished to exercise their religious loyalty.

Rationalists, thus, appear to have a choice: either accept faith as a beguiling but necessary aspect of human life, or seek to eradicate all forms of loyalty — religious, familial, social, and so on — and reap the consequences.

This brings us to the second point ignored by secular critics of faith, namely that faith is intrinsic to all moral theories. As the philosopher Richard Rorty points out there is no way of answering the question "Why not be cruel?" without engaging in a leap of faith, be it the "leap" of creating a concept of human rights, or the "leap" of developing a notion of secular humanism. Much as we would like to think otherwise, there is "no noncircular theoretic backup for the belief that cruelty is horrible".[30] Wittgenstein appeared to have reached the same conclusion when he wrote that, in order to achieve enlightenment, man had to "surmount" certain propositions. "He must so to speak throw away the ladder, after he has climbed up on it."[31]

That is not to say reason should be banished from the study of ethics. Rather, moral philosophers should be honest about the limits of rationality. Perhaps too they should recognise faith as the virtue it is. After all, without some continuity of thought, resilience of mind, or loyalty to belief, one is condemned to a life of equivocation and passivity, like the protagonist in the Aesopian fable of *The Boy and the Nettle*. By failing to act with conviction, take a leap of faith, and "grasp the nettle", the boy is stung over and over again, becoming a pathetic victim of circumstance.

Logic advises against grasping the nettle; the boy knows touching it stings. But doing the logical thing — the unfaithful thing — isn't always best. So the fable tells us, and it is not alone in doing so. Popular culture bombards us with messages about the value of "mind over matter", or "thinking oneself into doing". The drinks company Guinness recently ran an advertising campaign revolved around the single word, "Believe", and coupled it with images of extraordinary human endeavours.

Such secular sermonising celebrates one brand of faith, and there are many others. But what they all share in common is a belief — a sustained, unshakeable belief — in the unbelievable. Such is faith: holding firm to one's convictions when all the evidence — the probability of failure, for example, or the likelihood of persecution — says otherwise.

Rationalists may balk at the idea but faith is perhaps needed today more than ever. In a world of seemingly intractable conflict, endemic poverty, and insurmountable injustice, is there any virtue more urgently required than sustained, unshakeable belief in the possibility of change? Is there anyone more desperately needed than a Confucius, someone once described as "the one who knows a thing cannot be done and still wants to do it"?[32]

Where rationalist critics of faith have a point is where they criticise extreme zealousness, or *blind faith* — but in this they are not alone. Were they to open their eyes, they would find support for their case within the very religions they condemn.

Confucius, for example, said faith should be tempered by four other virtues — wisdom, propriety, righteousness, and *jen* (human-heartedness). Loyalty to belief did not define the Superior Man, said Confucius, and in doing so, the philosopher echoed the words of Jesus. The latter said:

> Take the case, my brothers, of someone who has never done a single good act but claims that he has faith. Will that faith save him? If one of the brothers or one of the sisters is in need of clothes and has not enough food to live on, and one of you says to them, 'I wish you well: keep yourself warm and eat plenty,' without giving them these bare necessities of life, then what good is that? Faith is like that: if good works do not go with it, it is quite dead.[33]

In Islam, faith is also inextricably linked to good works. As one textbook on Islamic morals puts it:

> The notion of "proper" conduct may not, in Islam, be separated from the notion of "good" deeds, nor from "faith" and "devotion". Faith and good deeds are both necessary in this world for a prosperous and ideal so-

ciety in which there is mutual and shared responsibility. And in the Hereafter, faith and good deeds are
the necessary conditions for forgiveness and salvation,
for admission to Paradise.[34]

What each religion acknowledges is that faith, notwithstanding
its importance, should sometimes yield to other virtues. If a
believer encounters someone in need, for example, he or she
should offer help rather than mere prayers. By so demonstrating charity, the believer does not abandon faith but rather opts
to prioritise another virtue in that particular instance.

But charity is not the only virtue to which faith should
sometimes yield. Audacity is another, and it is to it we now
turn.

Endnotes

[1] Adapted from Khattab, H. (1987), *Stories from the Muslim World*, London:
Macdonald, pp. 26-7.

[2] *The Analects* 2:5.

[3] *The Analects* 4:18.

[4] Richards, C. (1997), *Illustrated Encyclopaedia of World Religions*, Dorset:
Element Books, p. 75.

[5] *The Great Learning* 9.

[6] Cua A.S. (1998), *Moral Vision and Tradition: Essays in Chinese Ethics*, Catholic University of America Press: Washington DC, pp. 296–7.

[7] *The Analects* 19:13.

[8] Gandhi, M.K. (1927), *An Autobiography: or The Story of My Experiments With
Truth*, Ahmedabad, India: Navajivan Trust, pp. 16–17.

[9] Gandhi, M.K., *op. cit.*, pp. 391–2.

[10] Ruthven, M. (1997), *Islam: A Very Short Introduction*, Oxford University
Press, pp. 88–9.

[11] Al-Qaradawi Y. (1994), *The Lawful and the Prohibited in Islam*, Indiana:
American Trust Publications, p. 232.

[12] Abu Laylah, M. (1999), *Faith, Reason and Spirit*, Cairo: Al-Falah Foundation, p. 111.

[13] Buckhardt, J.L. (1984), *Arabic Proverbs: or The Manners and Customs of the Modern Egyptians*, London: Curzon Press, p. 245.

[14] Exodus 20:1–17.

[15] Matthew 15:4.

[16] Matthew 22: 15–21.

[17] Küng, H. (2001), *The Catholic Church*, Weidenfeld and Nicolson, London, p. 183.

[18] John 20:24–29.

[19] Whyte, R. (1966), *Ten Stories from Islam*, Lahore: Pakistan Branch, Oxford University Press, pp. 20-21.

[20] Ruthven, M. (2005), *Fundamentalism*, Oxford University Press, p. 174.

[21] Matthew 10:37.

[22] Genesis 9:18.

[23] Bahgat, A. (1997), *Stories of the Prophets*, Cairo: Islamic Home Publishing & Distribution, p. 58.

[24] Nicholson R.A. (1969), *A Literary History of the Arabs*, Cambridge University Press, p. 27.

[25] Plotkin, A. (1993), *The Ethics of World Relgions*, New York: Mellen University Press, p. 60.

[26] Dalmiya, V. (2001), 'Dogged Loyalties: A Classical Indian Intervention in Care Ethics', in J. Runzo and N.M. Martin (eds), *Ethics in the World Religions*, Oxford: Oneworld, p. 295.

[27] *Bhagavad-Gita* III 35.

[28] Gray, J. (2004), *Heresies: Against Progress and Other Illusions*, London: Granta Books, p. 44.

[29] Singer, P. (2004), *One World, The Ethics of Globalization* (second edition). New Haven & London: Yale University Press, pp. 161-2.

[30] Rorty, R. (1989), *Contingency, Irony and Solidarity*, Cambridge University Press, p. xv.

[31] Wittgenstein, L. (1921), *Tractatus Logico-Philosophicus*, Proposition 6.54.

[32] *The Analects* 14:41.

[33] James 2:14-17.

[34] Al-Kaysi, M. I. (1986), *Morals and Manners in Islam*, Leicster, England: The Islamic Foundation, p. 20.

6

AUDACITY

The Lord said to Abraham, "There are terrible accusations against Sodom and Gomorrah, and their sin is very great. I must go down to find out whether or not the accusations which I have heard are true." . . . Abraham approached the Lord and asked, "Are you really going to destroy the innocent with the guilty? If there are fifty innocent people in the city, will you destroy the whole city? Won't you spare it in order to save the fifty? Surely you won't kill the innocent with the guilty. That's impossible! You can't do that. If you did, the innocent would be punished along with the guilty. That is impossible. The judge of all the earth has to act justly."

The Lord answered, "If I find fifty innocent people in Sodom, I will spare the whole city for their sake."

Abraham spoke again: "Please forgive my boldness in continuing to speak to you, Lord. I am only a man and have no right to say anything. But perhaps there will be only forty-five innocent people instead of fifty. Will you destroy the whole city because there are five too few?"

The Lord answered, "I will not destroy the city if I find forty-five innocent people."

Abraham spoke again: "Perhaps there will be only forty."

He replied, "I will not destroy it if there are forty."

Abraham said, "Please don't be angry Lord, but I must speak again. What if there are only thirty?"

He said, "I will not do it if I find thirty."

Abraham said, "Please forgive my boldness in continuing to speak to you, Lord. Suppose that only twenty are found?"

He said, "I will not destroy the city if I find twenty."

Abraham said, "Please don't be angry, Lord, and I will speak just once more. What if only ten are found?"

He said, "I will not destroy it if there are ten."

After he had finished speaking with Abraham, the Lord went away, and Abraham returned home.[1]

Organised religions have traditionally had a problem with audacity, for understandable reasons. On the face of it, audacity seems to be in direct conflict with faith, or loyalty to belief. The audacious question God — like Abraham in the biblical story above — while the faithful are loyal to God despite having doubts or questions about His judgement. What is clear from the story above, however, is that audacity and faith need not be in conflict. Far from it. Abraham showed how the virtue that Jews call *chutzpah* is not the enemy of faith but a supporting friend; it is not a licence to mock sacred belief but a healthy ability to challenge it. This, after, all, was the same Abraham who, according to scripture, had been willing to sacrifice his own son to prove his loyalty to God. The scriptural Abraham was the epitome of faithfulness. Yet he dared to question God. He was both loyal and audacious but at different times, or under different circumstances.

Abraham's example draws our attention to something about virtue in the world's major religions which is now worth highlighting. In each tradition, there is a trade-off between virtues. Certain virtues should yield to others depending on the situation. Just how we should manage this dilemma is addressed in the Epilogue. But what is clear from our examination of religious literature is that exemplary Jews, Christians, Muslims and so on practice more than one virtue. Like Abraham, they are loyal when faith is required, and audacious when chutzpah is called for.

It should be noted that the audacity displayed by Abraham is not doubt, nor disrespect. Nor is it apostasy, the rejection of faith. Rather, it is critical and conscientious reasoning within the realm of faith. Such reasoning not only acts as a check on unquestioning devotion but it helps to consolidate faith on the basis that beliefs that are tested and challenged are all the stronger.

Another role model for Jews in this regard is Job who challenged God to explain evil in the world. Pious and upstanding, Job lost all his children and property and was afflicted with a repulsive disease. Despite the temptations of Satan, he refused to renounce his faith. Finally, he broke his silence, however, and cursed the day on which he had been born. "God knows everything I do," said Job. "He sees every step I take. I swear I have never acted wickedly and never tried to deceive others. Let God weigh me on honest scales, and he will see how innocent I am."[2] God replied out of the storm:

> "Who are you to question my wisdom, with your ignorant, empty words? Stand up now like a man and answer the questions I ask you. Were you there

when I made the world? If you know so much, tell me about it . . ."

Job got no apology from God, nor an explanation as to why he had been so misfortunate. But he had dared to question, and as a result his faith had been strengthened. Job, of course, was merely following the example of Jacob, who "wrestled with God" symbolically and literally in scripture. As legend has it, the prophet was camping near the home of his brother, whom he had sinned against, when a man came "and wrestled with him until just before daybreak". Jacob was struck on the hip and wounded but refused to let go of the shadowy figure.

> The man said, "Let me go; daylight is coming."
> "I won't, unless you bless me," Jacob answered.
> "What is your name?" the man asked.
> "Jacob," he answered.
> The man said, "Your name will no longer be Jacob. You have struggled with God and with men, and you have won; so your name will be Israel."
> Jacob said, "I have seen God face to face, and I am still alive."[3]

"Israel", the name given to Jacob, literally translates as "he wrestles with God". A similar accolade of "it wrestles with God" might be awarded to the state of Israel — a unique voice in the Middle East but one with a penchant for causing outrage. Arguably the most brazen state in the world (something which can be seen as positive or negative), Israel has consolidated the place of audacity in Jewish culture.

A related influence in this regard is the history of persecution against the Jews, culminating most gruesomely in the *Shoah*, or Holocaust, of the last century. Following the example of the early prophets, Jews have more recently questioned God's compassion, asking how He could have allowed six million men, women and children of their faith to perish at the hands of the Nazis. According to Jewish folk memory, God was questioned within the death camps themselves.

> There is a story that one day in Auschwitz, a group of Jews put God on trial. They charged him with cruelty and betrayal. Like Job, they found no consolation in the usual answers to the problem of evil and suffering in the midst of this current obscenity. They could find no excuse for God, no extenuating circumstances, so they found him guilty and, presumably, worthy of death. The Rabbi pronounced the verdict. Then he looked up and said that the trial was over: it was time for the evening prayer.[4]

Wrestling with God became a moral imperative for survivors of the genocide, and it prompted the Holocaust scholar Irving Greenberg to conclude: "Nothing dare evoke our absolute, unquestioning loyalty, not even our God, for this leads to possibilities of SS loyalties."[5]

While the Holocaust may have brought such questioning to the fore, it had been present for centuries in Judaism — in tandem with centuries of oppression against Jews. A story goes that the Hasidic Rabbi Levi-Yitzhak of Berdichev (1740–1810) once interrupted the sacred Yom Kippur service in order to protest that, "whereas kings of flesh and blood protected their peoples, Israel was unprotected by her king in heaven". It is also told that the Rabbi once asked a tailor to speak of an argument he had had with God:

[The tailor replied:] "I told the Master of the Universe . . . today is the Day of Judgement. One must repent. But I didn't sin much. I took a little left-over cloth from the rich. I once drank a glass of brandy and ate some bread without washing my hands. These are all my transgressions. But *You*, Master of the Universe, how many are *Your* transgression? You have taken away small children who had not sinned. From others you have taken away the mothers of such children. But, Master of the Universe, I shall forgive You Your transgressions, and may You forgive mine, and let us drink *L'Hayyim* [to life]!"

That year Reb Levi-Yitzhaq proclaimed that it was this tailor with his argument who had saved the Jews. "Ah," he added, "but if I had been in his place, I would not have forgiven the Master of the World such great sins in return for a little left-over cloth. While I had Him, I would have asked that He send us His Messiah to redeem the World!"[6]

With this heritage of *chutzpah*, is it any wonder that Jews are disproportionately represented in the fields of science and literature, not to mention among the ranks of professional comedians? From Groucho Marx to Woody Allen, and Joan Rivers to Jerry Seinfeld, Jews have produced a particular brand of comedy that mirrors their faith: analytical and bold but not deliberately insulting. It is a form of comedy that sails close to the wind, constantly testing the bounds of orthodox acceptability, without — in the main — overstepping the mark. It often asserts a Jewish identity, while making fun of textbook Judaism; keeping the faith, in other words, while questioning it.

Compared to Judaism, other faiths have a strained relationship with audacity. Islam has traditionally been intolerant towards internal criticism. According to orthodox Muslim belief, apostasy is one of just three crimes for which capital punishment is justified, the other two being murder and adultery. In Christianity, meanwhile, the fault lines between churches can be traced to independent, or audacious, thinking. Had many Christians in the sixteenth century not ceased to accept the authority of the Pope, the Protestant Reformation would never have happened. Protestant churches have since divided and multiplied as believers interpret new meanings of the Bible for themselves. That has created a Catholic Church that can be somewhat sceptical of the benefits of independent thought. Although various popes down the centuries have rubbished the notion of papal infallibility, including John XXII who described it in 1324 as "the father of all lies", the Vatican clings to the doctrine as a means of keeping its clergy in line.[7]

Eastern faiths are perhaps more willing to accept audacity as a virtue. Hinduism goes so far as viewing "scepticism" as a positive disposition, paving the way for philosophic thought. Like Jews, Hindus believe that critical reasoning does not undermine faith but strengthens it. Without the audacity to question sacred beliefs, or challenge God's authority, faith will be nothing more than the dry recitation of doctrine. Ownership of faith requires testing belief, challenging it and adapting it. In this, Hindus appear to agree with Goethe when he said: "What you have inherited from your father, you must earn over again for yourselves or it will not be yours." The bottom line in Hinduism is that you must figure out for yourself how best to live ethically. "The Real is one," says the *Rig Veda*, "but the sages speak of it in different ways."[8]

On reflection, how different is this approach to that taken by Christianity or Islam? Many Christians, including many Catholics, believe they too must take ownership of their faith through critical reasoning rather than relying on inherited wisdom. Even the supposed conservative Pope John Paul II spoke of philosophy as "one of the noblest of human tasks". In his 1998 *Encyclical on the Relationship between Faith and Reason*, the then Pope said it was necessary to retain "the audacity to forge new paths in the search" for ultimate truth:

> On her part, the Church cannot but set great value upon reason's drive to attain goals which render people's lives ever more worthy. She sees in philosophy the way to come to know fundamental truths about human life. At the same time, the Church considers philosophy an indispensable help for a deeper understanding of faith and for communicating the truth of the Gospel to those who do not yet know it.[9]

Perhaps a more radical spirit of Christian audacity could be found in social justice campaigners like Martin Luther King, the left-leaning liberation theologians of South America and Jesuit peace activists like Father Daniel Berrigan. Arguably, their form of audacity is closer to the virtue Jesus himself practised when he boldly befriended society's outcasts and preached an unheard of message of loving one's enemy. Don't overlook, moreover, Jesus' plea in the Garden of Gethsemane, "My Father, if it is possible take this cup of suffering from me!";[10] nor, indeed, Christ's final recorded words:

> "*Eli, Eli, lema sabachthani?* My God, my God, why did you abandon me?"[11]

Even the Son of God queried his Father's authority; so the Bible tells us. In doing so, Jesus seemed to endorse the message of Abraham: keep the faith while questioning it.

As for Islam, there are signs of a revival in the tradition of *ijtihad*, or independent reasoning, among Muslims. The scope of such reasoning has traditionally been circumscribed, in part due to the nature of the Qur'an. While Christians accept the Bible to be a man-made document, Muslims believe their holy book to be the literal word of God, and as such it is not open to critical revision. Nonetheless, tradition decreed for hundreds of years that Muslims who reached high religious office, or underwent extensive religious training, were entitled to interpret the Qur'an — that is until Sunni *ulema*, or clerics, declared in or around the eleventh century that "the gates of *ijtihad* had been closed". Muslims were told from this date forward to practice *taqleed*, or "imitation" of then established doctrine, rather than its opposite *ijtihad*.

Not all Muslims, nor Muslim scholars, accepted the ruling, however, not least the Shi'a *ulema* of Iran. More significantly, reformist Muslims from both Sunni and Shi'a traditions have today embraced *ijtihad* as a saving grace for Islam, arguing that each Muslim should apply the disciplined use of independent reasoning in order to best appreciate the meaning of his or her faith. Examples of *ijtihad*, or at least a sprit of questioning, can be found in Islamic literature, not least in the story of Abraham's test of loyalty to God. Each of the Abrahamic religions — Judaism, Christianity and Islam — recall how the so-called Father of the Prophets was called upon by God to sacrifice his son: Isaac in the Bible, and Ishmael in the Qur'an. But whereas the Christian and Jewish Abraham got Isaac to build a fire, while pretending that they were going to sacrifice a lamb, the Muslim Abraham boldly told Ishmael of God's command, and asked: "What is thy view?" As it happened, Ishmael agreed to being sacrificed "if Allah so wills". (He was spared, like Isaac, by divine intervention.) Crucially, however, the child's consent was sought. As well as endorsing the need for independent reasoning, the Muslim story underlines a core aspect of Islamic belief, namely that becoming a Muslim is a voluntary act. According to orthodox teaching, religion which is spread by force is an offence against Islam.

A relatively more recent role model for audacious Muslims is Abdu'l-Walid Ibn Rushd, better known as Averroes (1126–1198). The leading philosopher to emerge from Muslim Spain during Islam's historic and, some say, "golden rule" of Iberia, Avorroes famously defended philosophy from claims that it was anti-Islamic. He admired the thinkers of ancient Greece, particularly Aristotle, whom he regarded as embodying the highest development of the human intellect. He defended the rights of women, arguing that society had reduced them to "vegetables". He believed that, while the Qur'an contained the highest truth, its words should not be taken literally. And he advocated a fusion between reason and faith that would inspire Saint Thomas Aquinas, and give impetus to the development of the scholastic and rationalist movements in Christian Europe. His views were so offensive to Islamic zealots, however, that they had him stoned in the great mosque of Cordoba. When fanatics destroyed a famous library in the city, Avorroes was reported to have exclaimed: "There is no tyranny on earth like the tyranny of priests."

Some moderate Muslims regret the absence of a period of rationalism, Reformation or Enlightenment in Islamic history, believing that what the religion needs most is a tradition of critiquing truth. As the French Algerian scholar Mohammed Arkoun remarked, "It is unfortunate that philosophical critique of sacred texts — which has been applied to the Hebrew Bible and the New Testament without engendering negative consequences for the notion of revelation — continues to be rejected by Muslim scholarly opinion."[12]

The violent reaction among educated Muslims to the publication of Salman Rushdie's novel *The Satanic Verses* in November 1988 demonstrated just how limited the scope for audacity is in Islam. The Somali-born Dutch parliamentarian Ayaan Hirsi Ali had to go into hiding after renouncing her faith on television, while Theo van Gogh, the director of a film which she wrote on the treatment of women in Islam, was murdered by a Muslim fanatic in November 2004. "Ibn Warraq", a prominent Muslim-born writer trained in Arabic, felt obliged to publish under a pseudonym because of the risk of attack, and it remains the case that Muslims worldwide run great risks to their health and welfare by leaving Islam, or criticising the religion openly. In supposedly moderate Malaysia, for example, Muslims who seek to convert to other religions are labelled apostates and packed off to rehabilitation camps. In Britain, some Muslims who have converted to Christianity have been "punished" with intimidation, violence and abuse.[13]

Depressing as these trends are, signs of a possible counter-movement in Islam are emerging. Demonstrating a fresh spirit of audacity, reformist students, and, in particular, women, are leading the campaign for change. Canadian

author Irshad Manji, who wrote a best-selling book on "the
trouble with Islam", has urged fellow young Muslims "to replace the *jihadists* with a new generation of '*ijtihadists*'".[14]
Someone like Shirin Ebadi, the Iranian lawyer and human
rights defender who won the 2003 Nobel Peace Prize, is em-
blematic of a new willingness to question religious orthodoxy.
So too is Iran's thriving film industry, whose recent commer-
cial successes include the taboo-breaking *Marmulak*, a comedy about a fugitive criminal disguised as a *mullah*.

Perhaps the best indicator of a fresh spirit of audacity
among Muslims is the revival of humour in Islamic popular
culture. Among an increasing number of Muslim comics
working in the UK is Shazia Mirza who performs in a *hijab*
and says she doesn't do jokes about sex because she has
never had it. She opened a show three weeks after 11 September with the line: "My name is Shazia Mirza, or at least
that is what is says on my pilot's licence."

Conservative Muslims find such humour distasteful, if not
blasphemous. But comedians like Mirza are following in a
time-honoured tradition of Arab storytellers and humorists.
Among the many comic folk tales in Arab literature is the following, a story relating to Djuha, the alter ego of Nasruddin
the Mullah, whom we shall meet in the chapter on Wisdom:

> When Djuha grew to be an old man, his friends
> began to admonish him with regard to his welfare in
> the next world. "You would do better to turn your
> thoughts to prayer rather than joke all the time," they
> said. "You should spend your days in serious medita-
> tion and in studying the *hadith*." "I have not neglected
> the utterances of the prophet," retorted Djuha, "I am
> sure that none of you has ever heard of the *hadith* of

Ikrimah." "Tell it to us," said his friends. "The learned
Ikrimah," began Djuha, "says that according to Ibn
Abbas, who had it from the prophet himself, there
are two qualities which can ensure happiness for the
faithful both in this world and the next." "Tell us what
they are," said his friends eagerly.

"Ikrimah forgot one," said Djuha, "and I have for-
gotten the other."[15]

Audacity is, thus, not the sole property of Jews. For moderate Muslims, and indeed moderate Christians, critical reasoning and the questioning of religious orthodoxy is to be
welcomed. Whether such "moderates" best represent their
respective religious traditions is open to debate. But Pope
John Paul II left Catholics in no doubt on the matter, saying
faith and independent reasoning were both to be embraced.
"Each influences the other, as they offer to each other a puri-
fying critique and a stimulus to pursue the search for deeper
understanding."[16]

As for Muslims, support for the notion of embracing *ijtihad* is seemingly given by no less a figure than Muhammad. In
a *hadith*, or episode attributed to the Prophet, his *qadi*, or
jurist, Muadh ibn Jabal argues — apparently with Muhammad's
imprimatur — that faith should not be blind to reason. The
hadith runs so:

Prophet: How will you decide a problem?
Muadh: According to the Qur'an.
Prophet: If it is not in it?
Muadh: According to the Sunnah (collection of Is-
lamic customs).
Prophet: If it is not in that either?
Muadh: Then I will use my own reasoning.[17]

The lesson carries as much, if not more, weight today. In a rapidly changing and complex world, we cannot depend upon literal interpretations of holy scripture to give us all the answers we need. Notwithstanding our faith, we have no choice but to be audacious and to think for ourselves.

Endnotes

1 Genesis 18: 20–33.

2 Job: 31: 2–6.

3 Genesis: 32:22–30.

4 Armstrong, K. (1999), *A History of God*, London: Vintage, p. 431.

5 Fashing, D.J. and Dechant D. (2001), *Comparative Religious Ethics*, Massachusetts: Blackwell Publishing, p. 64.

6 Lane, B. (1986), "Hutzpa K'Lapei Shamaya: A Christian Response to the Jewish Tradition of Arguing with God" in *Journal of Ecumenical Studies* 23, 4, 567–8, as quoted in Fashing, D.J. and Dechant D. *op. cit.*, p. 179.

7 Küng, H. (2001), *The Catholic Church*, Weidenfeld and Nicolson, London, p. 121.

8 For a commentary on scepticism in Hinduism see Radhakrishnan S. and Moore C.A. (eds) (1957), *A Sourcebook in Indian Philosophy*, New Jersey: Princeton University Press, p. 34.

9 *Fides et Ratio*, 15 September 1998, p. 3.

10 Matthew 26:39.

11 Matthew 27:45.

12 Ruthven, M. (2000), *Islam in the World*, New York: Oxford University Press, p. 383.

13 *The Times*, London, 5 February 2005, "Muslim apostates cast out and at risk from faith and family".

14 See: www.muslim-refusenik.com

15 Bushnaq, I. (1986), *Arab Folktales*, London & New York: Penguin Books, p. 258.

16 *Fides et Ratio*, p. 44.

17 Holm, J. (eds.) (1994), *Making Moral Decisions*, London & New York: Continuum, pp. 102–3.

7

HONESTY

Zeng Shen was a disciple of Confucius.

One day Zeng Shen's son was crying because his mother refused to let him go shopping with her.

"Be a good boy, and stay at home," said the mother. "When Father comes back, we are going to kill a pig and cook a nice meal for you. I know you like pork."

The boy nodded and stayed at home.

When she got back, she saw Zeng Shen ready to kill a pig in the family's pigsty. She hastened to stop him.

"I was only joking. You needn't kill the pig today."

"This is no joking matter," Zeng Shen said. "Make sure you never lie to a child. A child does not know what is right and what is wrong. He imitates his parents. Now if you deceive him, he will think that it is all right to deceive. And he will not believe you any more. This is not the way to teach a child."

Thus Zeng Shen killed the pig and cooked some pork for the boy.[1]

Lying is the most insidious of vices. Once a lie is born it grows legs — for a lie can only be sustained by another lie. If dishonesty takes hold in someone's character it becomes difficult, if not impossible, to shake it off. Hence the world's faiths put great store by truth-telling, particularly in children. From *The Boy Who Cried Wolf* to *Pinocchio*, boys and girls are reminded in no uncertain terms that honesty is indeed the best policy.

The story above acknowledges the corrupting influence of lies from a Confucian perspective. "Hold faithfulness and sincerity as first principles," said Confucius.[2] His disciple Zeng Shen duly obeyed. In Indian philosophy, few sins, if any, are worse than lying. The *Rig Veda*, one the earliest texts of Hindu literature, declares: "Wherever sin is found in me, whatever evil I have wrought, If I have lied or falsely sworn, Waters, remove it far from me."[3]

Honesty is similarly acclaimed in Buddhism, the virtue being described as one of "Five Precepts" for a boddhisattva, or religious devotee. "In certain cases, a bodhisattva may destroy life, take what is not given to him, commit adultery, drink strong drink, but he may not tell a lie," declares one Buddhist text.[4] Slander is particularly sinful under Buddhist teaching as it harms both the slanderer and the subject of his or her lies. "If you've nothing nice to say, say nothing at all," is the motto of the bodhisattva, who is described by the Buddha as "a bondman to truth, trustworthy, dependable, no deceiver of the world". The Buddha continues:

> Having heard something here he [the bodhisattva] is not one for repeating it elsewhere for [causing] variance among these [people] . . . In this way he is a

reconciler of those who are at variance, and one who combines those who are friends. Concord is his pleasure, concord his delight, concord his joy, concord is the motive of his speech.[5]

Stories from Indian folklore highlight the pernicious effects of slander. One such tale recalls:

There was once an ascetic named Harasvamin who fell victim to a rumour that he captured and ate children. Soon all the people in the town where he lived were avoiding him, and started hiding their children in their homes. Even the Brahmans ran when Harasvamin approached, much to his amazement. Eventually, Harasvamin asked why people were avoiding him.

"Because," the reply came, "You are eating the children here on sight."

Harasvamin said: "Why don't you consult among yourselves to see how many children I have eaten?"

So the Brahmans asked around, and discovered that every child in the town was still alive. Thereupon all the people declared: "Truly this worthy man has been falsely accused by us fools; everybody's children are alive, so whose has he eaten?"[6]

The crime of slander features prominently too in *The Fables of Bidpai*, a collection of stories first composed in India around 300 BCE but later assimilated into both Hindu and Islamic traditions. The central tale concerns the wicked jackal Dimnah, who sows discontent amongst his animal peers by spreading gossip and rumour. Tragedy ensues when the lion kills his one-time fried, the ox Shanzebah, on foot of

Dimnah's lies. Having "sowed tricks and reaped shame of face", Dimnah is condemned to "eternal torment" in prison.[7]

In light of such teachings, it could be argued that eastern faiths are more damning of slander than their western counterparts. Islam and Judaism both regard slander as a sin; the Qur'an assigns specific punishments for anyone who falsely accuses a married woman of wrongdoing, while the Torah instructs: "Do not go about as a tailbearer [slanderer] against your people"[8] — yet other forms of lying perhaps receive greater attention in both faiths. The Qur'an, for instance, goes into great detail on the need for honesty in business and commerce, detailing rules of fair trade for Muslims. The Talmud similarly lays down strict laws for Jews on the way they should conduct their business, noting: "The shopkeeper must wipe his measures twice a week, his weights once a week, and his scales after weighing." And, "You shall do no unrighteousness in judgement, in meteyard [land measurement], in weight or in measure."[9]

Stories are told about how scrupulous the early rabbis were in their dealings. For instance:

> It happened that Phineas was living in one of the cities in the South, and some men who visited there left two measures of barley in his possession and forgot about them when they departed. He sold the barley, and each year stored the produce. After seven years had elapsed, the men returned to the town. He recognised them and told them to take what belonged to them. It also happened that Simeon Ben Shetach bought an ass from an Arab. His disciples found a gem suspended around its neck and said to him: "Rabbi, it is true of you. The blessings of the

Lord are rich." He replied: "I bought the ass and not
the gem. Go, return it to the owner." The Arab exclaimed: "Blessed be the God of Simeon Ben
Shetach."[10]

Similar qualities can be found in Adham, a pious man of Islamic lore, who once — the story goes — spotted a peach
floating down the canal next to which he performed his daily
ablutions. Only when he had finished his prayers did he pluck
the fruit out of the water and eat it. Suddenly, however, Adham realised he had taken something which did not belong to
him. He followed the river upstream until he reached a peach
orchard, and there he produced two copper coins in payment
for the fruit. He insisted on paying despite the pleadings of a
princess who owned the orchard. In the course of their debate, she admitted that she did not own the garden alone.
Half of it belonged to her brother, the Sultan, who lived five
days' journey away. The story continues:

> Without hesitation, Adham took one of the coins
> back, greeted the princess politely, and left the peach
> garden. He took the direction of the capital, walking
> through the night and most of the next day and night,
> so that he arrived in three days, not in five. He re-
> quested an audience with the Sultan and was admitted
> the same evening. He explained to the Sultan that he
> owed him a copper coin for eating half a peach, and
> that he had travelled 40 hours to pay it. The Sultan,
> who was known for his wisdom, observed with atten-
> tion this man who insisted on paying for a fruit he had
> found floating in a river, and reflected on this rare oc-
> currence of scrupulous honesty.

Then the Sultan rose, told Adham to wait, and entered the interior rooms of his palace. There he found his daughter, his only child, who was a girl of difficult character. The Sultan spoke to her, "Tell me again, what sort of man you will be prepared to marry." She said: "Only a man who is absolutely honest in his dealings, righteous in his life, and scrupulous in obeying the law, will find favour in my eyes." So the Sultan answered her: "Prepare for your wedding then, for that man has just arrived, guided no doubt by God's council [*sic*]. You will not find one more honest or righteous in the kingdom."[11]

In another legend from the faith, Omar — the second Caliph of Islam — was once walking through the streets of Medina when he passed a small house where an old milkseller lived with her daughter. He heard the old woman say:

> "Daughter, you should add water to the milk before you sell it. Then the quantity will be twice as much, and we shall get twice as much money for it!"
>
> The girl replied, "Mother, that is wrong! The Caliph has said that water must not be added to milk which is for sale!"
>
> "I know, I know," said the old woman, "but the Caliph is not here to see what we do!"
>
> The girl said, "Even if the Caliph cannot see us, his orders must be obeyed. Allah sees us and everything that we do!"[12]

The milkseller's daughter was rewarded for her honesty by an offer of marriage to one of Omar's sons. But, like Adham, the girl hadn't sought recompense. Quite the reverse; both Adham and the milkseller's daughter told the truth even though it would have been easier, and less costly in a material sense, to tell a lie.

Here we alight upon an important aspect of honesty. The virtue is not performed by telling the truth when it suits one to do so. Honesty is, rather, telling the truth for its own sake.

Stories affirming this message can be found in all faiths. Take, for instance, the Islamic tale of Abdul Kadir, who owned up to thieves exactly how much money he had when he could have pretended to have had less. Or the Hindu legend of the life of Rama, who at great personal cost, refused to break a promise which he had previously made. "Truth is our ancient path," he told his tormentors. "Truth endures when all else passes away. The venom of falsehood is more deadly than the venom of a serpent's sting." Alluding to the offence caused by dishonesty, even if undiscovered, Rama asked: "Is a woman to consider herself a widow when her husband is out of sight? . . . Know, all of ye, that I will be faithful to the mandate of my sire. I will keep my promise which I cannot recall."[13]

Gandhi similarly endorsed the notion of truth-telling for its own sake, confessing in his autobiography to once letting his wife sneak into the second-class bathroom on a long train journey across India for which they had third-class tickets. Years later, he was still racked with guilt. "I knew that my wife had no right to avail herself of the second class bathroom, but I ultimately connived at the impropriety," he wrote. "This, I know, does not become a votary of Truth. Not that my wife was eager to use the bathroom, but a husband's partiality for his wife got the better of his partiality for Truth."[14]

Honesty within the world's major faiths means more, however, than merely refraining from telling lies. There is a positive dimension to the virtue in terms of "being true to oneself". Confucius described this quality as "sincerity", saying: "Only those who are absolutely sincere can fully develop their nature. If they can fully develop their nature, they can then fully develop the nature of others. If they can fully develop the nature of others, they can then fully develop the nature of things. If they can fully develop the nature of things, they can then assist in the transforming and nourishing process of Heaven and Earth. If they assist in the transforming and nourishing process of Heaven and Earth, they can thus form a trinity with Heaven and Earth."[15]

Others religious figures identify altogether more earthly benefits from honesty. Gandhi spoke of truth's liberating effects in his own life, recalling a confession he made to his dying father for a crime he committed in his youth. Gandhi had written on a slip of paper how he had stolen a gold armlet from his brother to pay for a smoking habit he had developed in his teens:

> In this note not only did I confess my guilt, but I asked adequate punishment for it, and closed with a request to him not to punish himself for my offence. I also pledged myself never to steal in future. . . . He read it through, and pearl-drops trickled down his cheeks, wetting the paper. For a moment he closed his eyes in thought and then tore up the note. He had sat up to read it. He again lay down. I also cried. I could see my father's agony. If I were a painter I could draw a picture of the whole scene today. It is still so vivid in my mind. Those pearl-drops of love cleansed my heart, and

washed my sin away. . . . I know that my confession
made my father feel absolutely safe about me, and increased his affection for me beyond measure."[16]

While honesty may be universally acclaimed by the world's
major religions, one must ask, however, whether it should
yield under certain circumstances to other virtues — like
justice or faith. In Plato's *Republic*, Socrates famously questioned the merits of telling the truth to a madman. Speaking
of the primacy of justice, the philosopher argued against returning a sword to someone who had lost his or her mind
since it had been borrowed. The tenth-century Islamic rationalist 'Abd al-Jabbar made a similar case for subverting
honesty to the demands of justice, claiming truth should be
avoided where it would endanger the life of the speaker, or
another person.[17] In much the same way, Confucius permit-
ted lying to despots and aggressors. "I do not keep promises
made under duress," he said. "Even God would disregard
such promises."[18] And, although Buddhism and Hinduism may
be less explicit on the subject, the *Mahabharata* appears to
allow justice take precedence over honesty when it states: "It
is always proper to speak the truth. It is better again to speak
what is beneficial than to speak what is true."[19]

It has traditionally been accepted, moreover, that truth is
a necessary first casualty of war. Sun Zi (died c. 500 BCE),
whose *Art of War* remains recommended reading in military
training schools, noted: "Warfare is essentially based on de-
ception, that is, to hide your real intention and keep the enemy guessing. When you are capable of attacking the enemy,
pretend that you are not. When you are actively making
preparations, pretend you are not."[20] Echoing such thoughts,

Winston Churchill remarked a year before D-Day: "Sometimes truth is so precious it must be attended by a bodyguard of lies."

But if justice should trump honesty on occasion, what about faith? Should one ever cling to a belief system that contains falsehoods? More precisely, should one ever believe something one knows not to be true?

Naturally, religious leaders tend to deny any contradiction between faith and honesty. In religious texts, the terms "truth" and "belief" are often interchangeable. Yet, within each tradition, there is an undeniable strain of mythology. The Catholic Church, for instance, rejects claims that *The Story of Creation* in Genesis is false without regarding it as literally true. God didn't actually create the world in seven days, nor did He make man in His physical image. Yet, in a mysterious or enigmatic sense, Genesis provides an accurate account of the creation of both man and earth; so the church teaches.

Atheists rubbish such thinking, and accuse the church of failing to face up to facts. They regard as disingenuous the Vatican's assertion that creationism is consistent with the theory of evolution, and cite as further proof of the "dishonesty" of Catholicism evidence suggesting that a minority of Catholics believe the Eucharist is actually the Body and Blood of Christ.[21] Atheist critics declare that the Catholic Church is riddled with falsehoods, and these cannot be wished away by converting them into myths.

Such objections bring into focus the following question: can we be honest while embracing mythology? If we treat a fictional story as though it were true, are we being dishonest? The question is of central importance to this book, as we are seeking to learn from myths and fables, stories which may not be factual but purport to contain certain truths. Rationalist critics of religion might argue that *The Story of Virtue* is a dishonest project in that is uses mythology to provide a justification for religious tradition. They might say that, in celebrating religious morality tales, it tells "white lies" in order to sustain a "black" one, namely the "lie" that there is truth in religion. But should mythology be condemned so hastily? If belief in a lie helps someone to live a better life, then why not let him or her believe? More to the point, could we do without mythology? Factualising fable may be not just desirable but necessary in moral frameworks. Plato acknowledged as much in *The Republic*, when he hailed the concept of "the noble lie" or "magnificent myth", a story with which the citizens of Athens could collectively identify. Although fictional, such a myth would be read as truth in Plato's idealised Republic to unite a diverse population in their endeavours. The philosopher had Socrates describe such a "noble lie" in which rulers, soldiers and the community at large:

> . . . were fashioned and reared, and their arms and equipment manufactured, in the depths of the earth, and Earth herself, their mother, brought them up, when they were complete, into the light of day; so now they must think of the land in which they live as their mother and protect her if she is attacked, while their fellow-citizens they must regard as brothers born of the same mother earth.[22]

The story continued in sympathy with Plato's endorsement of a hierarchical Republic, claiming that the ruling class was fashioned from gold, auxiliaries from silver and farmers and other workers from iron and bronze. Thus, "the first and most important of god's commandments to the Rulers is that in their exercise of their function as Guardians their principal care must be to watch the mixture of metals in the characters of their children."[23]

The notion of the "noble lie" has been attacked for inspiring pernicious nationalist myths like Rome's creative tale of Romulus and Remus, and, more recently, the perverse Nazi story of a Fatherland dominated by the Aryan race. However, the problem with "the noble lie" is perhaps not so much its intention as its scope. Who would object, for example, to a myth that transcended national boundaries, and inspired solidarity between all the world's people?

Arguably, we have such a myth already in the story of human beings being afforded natural and inalienable rights — rights which may well be desirable but are nonetheless, in the words of Jeremy Bentham, "nonsense upon stilts". In perhaps the most celebrated version of this story (a version provided by John Rawls), man is "born" behind a "veil of ignorance" which prevents him from having knowledge of his status in society. The Rawlsian tale goes that man in this "original position" chooses a set of laws which guarantees the rights of minorities and a relatively equal distribution of wealth.[24]

The original position is, of course, a fictional creation. Man doesn't legislate with a blindfold on; he is all too aware of his status in society. If he is rich he will tend to oppose taxes, and if he is poor he will tend towards the reverse. If he is part of a majority grouping he may care little about the rights of minorities, and if he is part of a minority he may care a great deal more. Rawls, thus, was selling us a lie. But arguably it was — and is — a "noble lie", a lie that we should accept as though it were true. By pretending to dwell behind the veil of ignorance we may become better people, and create a more ethical society.

Rawls was not the first western philosopher to invent a myth of creation that might be capable of replacing religious fables like those contained in Genesis. Thomas Hobbes imagined man to have inhabited a primitive and terrifying state of nature prior to the establishment of government. Rousseau and Marx, in contrast, idealised the state of nature, arguing that man was inherently good but corrupted by either civilisation or economic exploitation. The English biochemist James E. Lovelock scrapped the modern assumption that man could be separated from nature, arguing that we inhabit a self-regulating system, or meta-organism, in the Earth. According to his theory of *Gaia*, which harks back to man's primordial religion, animism, we should take care of our physical environment as we are merely one of many species inhabiting a greater being.

For all their imaginative effort, however, thinkers such as Hobbes, Rousseau and Lovelock have plainly failed to produce a sufficiently convincing creation myth to dislodge time-honoured favourites like *The Garden of Eden* and *The Story of Creation* from Genesis in the minds of religious believers. Such stories may be unfactual — and so too creation myths in other faiths — but they continue to inspire believers to see themselves as part of a universal family and, in that, surely they do some good.

Mythology, thus, has its benefits. Leaving religion aside, consider how parents use fictional characters to inculcate virtuous behaviour in their children. Santa Claus rewards obedience, for example, and the Tooth Fairy bravery. Each character is an invention but both are spoken of as though they existed. It is true parents could probably do without such myths. But if they did, would they not have to create new stories?

Parents could, for instance, tell their children that "virtue brings its own reward", or that "good things happen to good people". Yet neither statement is strictly true. Vice can be more rewarding than virtue, and good people may perish at the expense of bad. The question, thus, arises: why create a myth of dubious efficacy when we can embrace one that definitely works — a myth, for example, like *The Boy Who Cried Wolf*, the most paradoxical of morality tales. In recounting the story as though it were true, we effectively tell a lie in order to encourage honesty. But what more vivid description can we give of the perils of falsehood?

Admittedly, it is a personal decision as to whether a myth is "noble" or not. Some may criticise *The Boy Who Cried Wolf* for using fear to inspire truth-telling, just as some may criticise *The Story of Creation* for making the notion of a universal humanity contingent on the existence of God. On a broader level, people may disagree over which religious tradition is true, or truer, among the various possibilities.

Is Islam more honest than Christianity? Is Buddhism more honest than Confucianism? We all have to answer such questions for ourselves. But, in their celebration of common virtues, the world's major religious traditions could well be seen not as competing falsehoods but as different versions of a magnificent myth, and of perhaps the noblest of lies.

Endnotes

1 Tang, C. (1996), *A Treasury of China's Wisdom*, Beijing: Foreign Languages Press, p. 89.

2 *The Analects* 1:8.

3 *Rig Veda* 22.

4 Garrett Jones, J. (1979), *Tales and Teachings of the Buddha*, London: George Allen & Unwin, p. 89.

5 Garrett Jones, J., *op. cit.*, p. 120–1.

6 Gray, J.E.B. (1961), *Indian Tales and Legends*, Oxford University Press, p. 34-5.

7 Keith-Falconer, I.G.N. (1885), *Kalilah and Dimnah: or The Fables of Bidpai*, Cambridge University Press, pp. 63–4.

8 *VaYikra* (Leviticus) 19:16.

9 Plotkin, A. (1993), *The Ethics of World Religions*, New York: Mellen University Press, p. 56.

10 Plotkin, A., *op. cit.*, p. 57.

11 Knappert, J. (1985), *Islamic Legends*, The Netherlands: E.J. Brill, pp. 393–5.

12 Whyte, R. (1966), *Ten Stories from Islam*, Lahore: Pakistan Branch, Oxford University Press, pp. 28–9.

13 Mackenzie D.A. (1913), *Indian Myth and Legend*, London: Gresham Publishing, p. 399.

14 Gandhi, M.K. (1927), *An Autobiography*, Ahmedabad, India: Navajivan Trust, p. 321.

15 *The Doctrine of the Mean*, 22.

16 Gandhi, M.K., *op. cit.*, pp. 23–4.

17 Hourani G.F. (1971), *Islamic Rationalism: The Ethics of 'Abd al-Jabbar*, Oxford: Clarendon Press, p. 108.

18 Tang, C., *op. cit.*, p. 64.

19 *Santiparva* 329.13.

20 Tang, C., *op. cit.*, pp. 106–7.

21 According to a 1992 Gallup/Saint Augustine Center Association poll, only 30 percent of the respondents said Holy Communion was "really and truly. . . . the Body and Blood, Soul and Divinity of the Lord Jesus Christ". In a 1994 New York Times/CBS News poll, almost two-thirds of respondents said the Eucharistic bread and wine could be best understood as "symbolic reminders of Christ" rather than evidence of his real presence.

[22] Plato 414–5 in Lee, D. (translator) (1974), *The Republic*, Middlesex: Penguin, p. 181.

[23] *The Republic*, 415b.

[24] Rawls, J. (1999), *A Theory of Justice* (Revised Edition), Massachusetts: Belknap Press.

HUMILITY

The fox is a past master of flattery and cunning. One day he saw a raven settling on a tree, with a piece of meat in its beak. The fox sat down under the tree, looked up to the raven and began to praise him.

"Your colour," he began, "is pure black; that shows that you have the wisdom of Lao-tse [Lao Tzu] who knows how to preserve his obscurity. The manner in which you feed your mother proves your filial piety equals Master Chung's [Confucius'] solicitude for his parents. Your voice is harsh and strong; that shows that you possess the courage of King Hsiang who turned his enemies to flight by the mere sound of his voice. You are indeed the king of birds."

The raven was delighted to hear this and said: "You're too kind!"

And before he knew it he had dropped the piece of meat from his opened beak.

The fox caught it, ate it up, laughed and said: "Remember this, my friend: Whenever anyone sings your praises without cause you may be sure he is after something."[1]

Humility is as ancient a virtue as it is unfashionable. Some of
the oldest moral fables from across the globe issue the same
warning as the story above, a tale from Chinese folklore:
"Pride before a fall." It is perhaps the most recurrent lesson in
Aesop's Fables, that great standard-bearer of old-fashioned morality. Within the collection of fables — a collection traditionally used in tandem with religious instruction in Christianity,
Buddhism, and other faiths — one finds a version of the story
above.[2] But one also finds a range of other tales affirming the
same lesson. One hears of an oak tree boasting of its superiority to a reed only to find itself blown over in a storm. One
hears of a frog which literally bursts with pride as its tries to
compare itself to an ox. And one hears of the "vain jackdaw"
which sticks peacock feathers to its body to "the chastisement
of [its] betters and also the contempt of [its] equals".[3] The
stories are as unsubtle in their imagery as they are unambigu-
ous in their moral instruction. And further examples are not
hard to find in the literature of specific religions.

Take this tale, for instance, from Islamic lore, which relates to King Solomon — reputed to be so wise that he could
understand the language of animals:

> One day the king of the ants complained to Solo-
> mon that the elephant trampled on all the ants that
> came under his feet, and would not listen to the ap-
> peals of the ant-king. Solomon spoke to the elephant,
> admonishing him to look out where he placed his feet
> and not to step on ants if he could help it, but the
> elephant merely answered: "What do ants matter?
> What can they do to me?" So the king of the ants de-
> cided to teach the elephant a lesson: he assembled all
> his subjects and ordered them to dig a deep pit, large

enough to accommodate an elephant. This they covered with long but light branches, leaves and garden
stalks. The pit was made in one night on a spot where
the elephant used to pass every morning on his way
to his daily bath in the river. Sure enough, at dawn,
the elephant came walking down his path and tumbled
down into the pit. He never got out. The ants crept
into his body and devoured him from the inside.
Solomon spoke to the braggers: "Watch the ants, you
men of pride, and be humble!"[4]

Stories warning against vanity predate all of the world's main
religions. In ancient Egypt and pagan Europe under the Celts
belief was widespread in the "evil eye" — a legend which decreed that anything subjected to a jealous glare was cursed.
The English scholar of Arabia, Edward Lane (1801–1876) observed the legacy of this superstition during his stay in Islami-
cised Egypt:

On first arriving in Egypt he [Lane] was struck by
the incongruity of delicate ladies in glistening silk
scented with musk accompanied by dirt-smeared children clad in rags, until he learned that maternal affection, not indifference, explained the manner. Unkempt
children in public would be less likely to draw admiring and covetous looks which could maim and kill.
When a boy passed through the streets in his circum-
cision ceremony, he wore female ornaments to divert
the evil eye from his person and concealed part of his
face with an embroidered handkerchief for the same
purpose. At meals with invited guests, the partakers
uttered expressions to avert the evil eye, mindful of
the saying that "in the food that is coveted [i.e. upon
which an envious eye has fallen] there is no blessing".

. . . Failure to observe these precautions might lead to accidents or misfortunes. A friend related to Lane how he heard a woman remark, on seeing two very large jars of oil borne by a camel, "God preserve us! What large jars!" The camel driver failed to tell her to bless the Prophet, and a few minutes later the camel fell and broke both jars and one of its legs.[5]

Islam does not formally endorse the legend of the "evil eye". But it is sympathetic to its aim. According to one textbook on Islamic morals:

The most inclusive characteristics of the ideal Muslim personality are humility, modesty and simplicity or naturalness [lack of affectation]. Pride and arrogance in any aspect of conduct are not accepted, as no individual is superior to another except in his degree of faith and contribution of good deeds. Thus, clothes that show haughtiness, that flaunt social status, are forbidden. Manners in eating should demonstrate humility before the occasion as well as respect for the meal: leaning on a cushion while eating is forbidden. Sitting on the floor when eating is a sign of humility, and therefore recommended. Furnishings should show modesty and restraint; for example, the bed should not be set too high above the ground. Gait in walking, manner of address in greeting and in speech generally, should avoid any taint of arrogance.[6]

Under orthodox Islamic teaching, certain luxuries, such as the wearing of gold, or silk, by men, are banned outright. There is, as one Muslim scholar remarks:

. . . a social aim underlying these prohibitions. . . . From the Qur'anic point of view, luxurious living

leads to weakness among nations and to their even-
tual downfall; the existence of luxury is also an expression of social injustice, as only a few can afford
luxurious items at the expense of the deprived
masses of the people.[7]

Fondness of luxury, arrogance and vanity all breach the Islamic moral code, a code based on surrendering humbly to
the authority of Allah. The most common refrain in Muslim
discourse is "*Inshallah*", or "if God so wills". In Islam, all plans
and ambitions are subject to the same divine clause. Muslims
are reminded of this fact in daily conversations, in prayer, and
in morality tales.

One Iraqi folktale tells of a man's two daughters, the
older scheming, and the younger pious. It is recalled that the
father asked: "From where did my riches come?" The older
replied, "From you and your labours, father." But the
younger answered, "From God! It is the Lord who gives, and
it is the Lord who deprives." Sure enough, the younger
daughter was rewarded by Allah, and the older punished.[8]

Not all folktales are so straightforward, however. A
common theme of Arab literature is the punishing of children
who bring shame on their families. In such stories, a proud
parent, or sibling, is purported to be justified in carrying out
an "honour killing" of the offending party who, more often
than not, is female. Explaining the logic behind such killings,
one expert in Arab folklore remarks: "Protecting female
sexuality [that is, male honour] is the most important value in
Arab society, on which the family's sense of honour, its integ-
rity, and its self-respect all hinge. If a female were a willing
participant in an illicit relationship, she would be considered a

great offender, a traitor to the honour of the family . . . and her punishment could be severe. . . "9

Of course, the practice of "honour killings" is by no means confined to the world of folklore. It remains a feature of some Arab and Islamic societies, although its exact prevalence is a matter of some debate. The United Nations Population Fund has estimated that up to 5,000 women are the victims of "honour killings" worldwide each year. However, moderate Muslims see no place for it in Islam, regarding it as an unwelcome relic of the Age of Ignorance, the era preceding the arrival of the Prophet Muhammad.

In this age, known to Mulsims as *Jaheliyah*, pride was the first of all virtues. Bragging Bedouin warriors like Antar, or the Arab fighters of *The Story of Dhat al-Himma* who preferred to have their heads cut off than have their beards shaved by captors, were the heroes of the day.10 Muhammad changed that, not only by creating new norms of conflict-resolution (to be discussed in the chapter on Justice) but, by preaching against boastfulness and envy. Critically, he urged Muslims to be humble about displays of piety as well as wealth.

"Neither speak thy Prayer aloud, nor speak it in a low tone, but seek a middle course between," the Qur'an states.11 "And be moderate in thy pace, and lower they voice; for the harshest of sounds without doubt is the braying of an ass."12 In short, good Muslims should be humble about their own holiness. Hence, the Arab proverb, "The saint is an impostor."13

The point is reinforced in a story referred to in the Qur'an, in which Allah rebukes two angels for bragging about their supposed virtue.14 According to legend, Allah orders the pair to live on earth, under the names Harut and Marut, "until you have learnt how hard it is to prevent yourselves from sinning". The story goes that not long after arriving on earth the pair started lusting after a woman called Zuhara who, one night, asked them to share with her a glass of wine. Harut and Marut accepted, thinking it "such a minor sin". But before long they were drunk, and sleeping not just with her but with a neighbour whose husband was away. Moreover, the pair started worshipping a statue of Zuhara's god — a naked boy. So their debauchery continued until the neighbour's husband returned and threatened to inform the authorities. Harut and Marut beat him until he died, and then spread a rumour in town that he was a robber who had at-tacked them. The story continues:

> When they had sworn this in court before the judge, hoping to escape suspicion, it pleased the Lord to call them back from Earth. Their bodies were left behind, lying on the ground, while their spirits stood again before the high Throne. "I have ended your lives on Earth," spoke the Lord, "because it seemed to Me you had sinned enough. You failed to keep even one of My Commandments. You have now learnt how hard a man's life is since man has to keep My Ten Commandments and you could not even obey five of them." Harut and Marut were condemned to hang by their feet in a huge cave somewhere in a mountainous region on earth . . .[15]

Once again, the ageless lesson is affirmed: pride before a fall.

Other faiths share the same view of humility — that it must extend from ordinary human chores to how one prac-tises one's religion. A popular saying of Hasidic Judaism goes: "A person should always carry two pieces of paper in his/her pockets. On one should be written, 'For me the world was created', and on the other, 'I am but dust and ashes'."[16]

Gandhi, as a representative of Hinduism, spoke of man's need to reach "the farthest limit of humility". Although aware of his reputation as a holy man, or *Mahatma* (great soul), he said: "The world's praise fails to move me, indeed it very often stings me. . . . I must reduce myself to zero. So long as a man does not of his own free will put himself last among his fellow creatures, there is no salvation for him."[17]

As for Confucianism, humility is inextricably linked to the "Way of Heaven". Said Confucius:

> In archery we have something resembling the Way of the superior man. When the archer misses the centre of the target, he turns around and seeks for the cause of failure within himself.[18]

More pointedly, the Confucian *Doctrine of the Mean* says the superior man "does not display his virtue". In continues:

> The *Book of Odes* [a collection of Confucian poems and songs] says, "Over her brocaded robe, she wore a plain and simple dress," for she disliked the loudness of its colour and patterns. Thus the way of the superior man is hidden but becomes more prominent every day, whereas the way of the inferior man is conspicuous but gradually disappears. It is characteristic of the superior man to be plain, and yet people do not get tired of him. He is simple and yet rich in cultural adornment. He is amiable and yet systematically methodical. He knows what is distant begins with what is near. . . . The *Book of Odes* says, "I will cherish your brilliant virtue, which makes no great display in sound

or appearance." Confucius said, "In influencing people, the use of sound or appearance is of secondary importance." The *Book of Odes* says, "His virtue is as light as hair. . . . The operations of Heaven have neither sound nor smell."[19]

This is one of the greatest areas of convergence between Confucianism and Taoism. According to Lao Tzu, arrogance was a sign that one's advancement had reached its extreme limit. He said:

> The gentleman of the low type, on hearing the Truth, laughs loudly at it. If he had not laughed, it would not suffice to be the truth.[20]

Echoing the Confucian idea that virtue "makes no great display", Lao Tzu continued:

> The sage, putting himself in the background, is always to the fore. Remaining outside, he is always there. . . . He does not show himself; therefore he is seen everywhere. He does not define himself; therefore he is distinct. He does not assert himself; therefore he succeeds. He does not boast of his work; therefore he endures. He does not contend, and for that reason no one in the world can contend with him.[21]

In a foreboding tone, shared by other great prophets, the father of Taoism added: "To know how to be content is to avoid humiliation; to know where to stop is to avoid injury."[22]

In all faiths, it seems, the worst — and most dangerous — form of pride is that over one's supposed piety. To be beaten at the race-track or in the fashion stakes, having boasted about one's athleticism or style, is one form of shame. But it is a worse, and altogether more painful, ignominy to discover one is deluding oneself about one's own moral worth. In Christianity, the warning is perhaps best-phrased in Luke's Gospel which recalls Jesus visiting the home of a leading Pharisee, where he noticed how some of the guests were choosing the best seats. Jesus said:

> When someone invites you to a wedding feast, do not sit down in the best place. It could happen that someone more important than you has been invited, and your host, who invited both of you, would have to come and say to you, "Let him have this place." Then you would be embarrassed and have to sit in the lowest place. Instead, when you are invited, go and sit in the lowest place, so that your host will come to you and say, "Come on up, my friend, to a better place." This will bring you honour in the presence of all the other guests. For everyone who makes himself great will be humbled, and everyone who humbles himself will be made great.[23]

The parable, of course, is more than a lesson in party etiquette. It is a statement of God's intent. Jesus followed the above by telling his host to surround himself with "the poor, the crippled, the lame, and the blind" rather than the supposedly great and good. "God will repay you on the day the good people rise from death," Jesus said.

The warning is clear within the Christian framework: those smugly satisfied about their own virtue are in for a humiliating shock on Judgement Day. As for those who are humble, according to Jesus, "they will inherit the earth".[24]

Thus, humility is universally celebrated by the world's major religions; not that this should cause us any surprise. One of the consequences of believing in an omnipotent and divine god is that one isn't all-powerful, nor godly, oneself. As one is under the spell of a higher being, who will eventually cast judgement on one's behaviour, it is at the very least prudent to be modest.

What of the non-religious, however? Is there any reason to be humble if one doesn't believe in the "evil eye", divine punishment for pride, or any other such "superstition"?

In fact, there may well be. Experience tells us that the timeless lesson of "pride before a fall" stands up to reasoned scrutiny. "Be nice to people on the way up," it is often said, "because you'll meet them on the way down again."

Perhaps there is no way of proving that modesty is the best policy. But observing life's constant unpredictability, the human cycle of success and failure, and the levelling effects of ageing and ill-health, is surely enough to convince us that, even if we give up on God, we shouldn't give up being humble.

Endnotes

[1] Osers, E. (translator), (1971), *Chinese Folktales*, London: G. Bell & Sons, p. 23.

[2] Rhys, E. (ed.) (1928), *Aesop's Fables*, London: J.M. Dent & Sons, p. 7.

[3] Rhys, E. (ed.) op. cit., p. 11.

[4] Knappert, J. (1985), *Islamic Legends*, The Netherlands: E.J. Brill, p. 160.

[5] El-Shamy, H.M. (1980), *Folktales of Egypt*, University of Chicago Press, pp. xxix-xxxi.

[6] Al-Kaysi, M.I. (1986), *Morals and Manners in Islam*, Leicster, England: The Islamic Foundation, p. 19.

[7] Al-Qaradawi, Y. (1994), *The Lawful and the Prohibited in Islam*, Indiana: American Trust Publications, p. 84.

[8] El-Shamy, H.M. (1999), *Tales Arab Women Tell and the Behavioral Patterns They Portray*, Bloomington & Indianapolis: Indiana University Press, p. 280.

[9] Muhawi, I. and Kanaana, S. (1989), *Speak Bird, Speak Again: Palestinian Arab Folktales*, University of California Press, p. 33.

[10] Lyons, M.C. (1995), *The Arabian Epic: Heroic and Oral Story-telling* (Vol 1), Cambridge University Press, p. 34.

[11] The Qur'an 17:110.

[12] The Qur'an 31:19.

[13] Buckhardt, J.L. (1984), *Arabic Proverbs*, London: Curzon Press, p. 44.

[14] The Qur'an 2: 102

[15] Knappert, J. (1985), *op. cit.*, pp. 59–63.

[16] Rabbi Bunam quoted in Dorff, E.N. (2003), "A Jewish Perspective on Human Rights" in J. Runzo, N.M. Martin and A. Sharma (eds.), *Human Rights and Responsibilities in the World Religions*, Oxford: Oneworld, p. 212.

[17] Gandhi, M.K. (1927), *An Autobiography*, Ahmedabad, India: Navajivan Trust, p. 420.

[18] *The Doctrine of the Mean* 14.

[19] *The Doctrine of the Mean* 33.

[20] The Lao Tzu 41.

[21] The Lao Tzu 7 and 22.

[22] The Lao Tzu 45.

[23] Luke 14:7–14.

[24] Matthew 5:3–12.

9

TOLERANCE

Once Moses overheard a shepherd talking. It sounded as if the shepherd were talking to an uncle or a friend, but he was talking to God.

"I would like to help you, wherever you are, wash your clothes, pick lice from you, kiss your hands and feet at bedtime. . . ."

Moses was very upset. "Are you talking in such a way to the very creator of heaven and earth? Don't you have more respect?"

The shepherd hung his head and wandered off, saddened. But God came to rebuke Moses, saying:

"What's wrong for one person is right for another. Your poison can be someone else's honey. I don't care about purity or diligence in worship. Or impurity and sloth. They mean nothing to me. I am above all that.

"One way of worshipping is as good as another. Hindus do Hindu things. Muslims in India do what they do. It is all praise, and it is all right . . ."[1]

Historically, the relationship between tolerance and religion has been somewhat contradictory. Religious practitioners have been both the victims and perpetrators of intolerance. The persecution of the Jews by Nazi Germany made the right to freedom of religious worship, and "freedom of opinion and expression" a cornerstone of the United Nations Declaration of Human Rights.[2] Yet today many people, particularly those from a non-religious background, believe that these rights should be curtailed because of crimes carried out in the name of religion.

The author Sam Harris writes in the wake of the 9/11 al-Qaeda terrorist attacks, "Given the link between belief and action, it is clear that we can no more tolerate a diversity of religious beliefs than a diversity of beliefs about epidemiology and basic hygiene."[3] Paradoxically, however, he cites as one of the main faults of religion its intolerance, arguing that the sacred texts of the world's major religions "are in perverse agreement on one point of fundamental importance . . . 'respect' for other faiths, or for the views of unbelievers, is not an attitude that God endorses." Harris continues:

> While all faiths have been touched, here and there, by the spirit of ecumenicalism, the central tenet of every religious tradition is that all others are mere repositories of error or, at best, dangerously incomplete. Intolerance is thus intrinsic to every creed. Once a person believes — really believes — that certain ideas can lead to eternal happiness, or to its antithesis, he cannot tolerate the possibility that the people he loves might be led astray by the blandishments of unbelievers. Certainty about the next life is simply incompatible with tolerance in this one.[4]

A neuroscientist with a training in philosophy, Harris speaks
for a generation of scientific thinkers who see religion as the
main cause of conflict in the world. His thesis has been endorsed by such vanguards of latter-day rationalism as Peter
Singer, Alan Dershowitz and Richard Dawkins. But is he
right? Is tolerance incompatible with religious belief?

What is certain is that some faiths, more than others, encourage their followers to be tolerant. Jainism, a religion of
the Buddhist family, is perhaps most emphatic in embracing
the virtue. Jains advocate not just a physical accommodation
of man with other animals, balking at the taking of any life, but
an intellectual accommodation of different human ideas. Under the doctrine of "multiplism", Jains believe "no single
truth-telling 'point of view' can present a total or determinate
description of reality". Rather, autonomous truths "together,
integratively, constitute a totality".[5] In practice, this means
one can believe both a particular thing and its reverse without being inconsistent. Such thinking is explained with the
following example:

> A man has spinal curvature but wishes to join the pal-
> ace guards. An orthopaedist specialising in this condi-
> tion measures him along the spine when collecting
> data and finds him six feet tall. But when he goes to
> see the sergeant-major of the guards, the latter makes
> him stand on the parade ground and measures him at
> his shoulder, and finds him less than six feet tall. . . .
> There is a difference in point of view, and the differ-
> ence is non-trivial. In that case, the Jaina would say
> that the man is and is not six feet tall, say that without
> contradiction, and yet say something interesting about
> the manifoldness of reality.[6]

Jain thinking has its problems, however. How does it differ from the faithless philosophy of relativism? Could it be equated to the Orwellian concept of *doublethink*, defined as "the power of holding two contradictory beliefs in one's mind simultaneously, and accepting both of them"?[7] Moreover, Jain "tolerance" is open to the charge that it is not tolerance at all. Tolerance is a willingness to allow different views to be expressed, crucially, when those views cause offence, or clash with one's own outlook. In Jainism, contradictory views do not create such a clash but an opportunity for reaching a better understanding of reality. If no offence is caused, where is the toleration? As one author points out, the Jain outlook "is not what we normally understand as toleration". Rather, it is "toleration in a special, very strong sense, for it is vital for the Jaina to be able to hold that the conclusions of both [opposing] views are assertible, each given a circumscribed viewpoint."[8]

Other eastern faiths come close to endorsing Jain "tolerance". Gandhi argued that "rival" religions were merely "different roads converging on the same point". "What does it matter that we take different roads," he asked, "so long as we reach the same goal? In reality, there are as many religions as there are individuals."[9] Describing mutual toleration as "the golden rule of conduct", he preached that because "we are imperfect ourselves, religion as conceived by us must also be imperfect." As Hindu–Muslim tensions spilled over into rioting in India, Gandhi adopted the catch-cry of "*Ishwara Allah tera nam*", or "*Ishwara* and Allah are both your names, O Lord". He later wrote:

> There is in Hinduism room for Jesus, as there is for Mohammed, Zoroaster and Moses. For me the differ-

ent religions are beautiful flowers from the same garden, or they are branches of the same majestic tree.
Therefore they are equally true, though being received and interpreted through human instruments
equally imperfect.[10]

Sufi Muslims endorse this view. The influential Jalal ad-Din
Rumi (1207–73) said God could not be understood, nor wor-
shiped, objectively. The author of "the Sufi Qur'an", the
Mathnawi, from which the story which opened this chapter is
taken, Rumi believed in one God but argued that our conception of Him was necessarily varied. The philosophy was contained in perhaps his most famous poem:

> Come, Come again! Whatever you are . . . Whether
> you are infidel, idolater or fireworshipper. Whether
> you have broken your vows of repentance a hundred
> times. This is not the gate of despair; This is the gate
> of hope. Come, come again . . .[11]

Tolerance, so understood, is a form of intellectual modesty,
or non-judgementalism. In his autobiography, Gandhi gave the
practical example of a lucky charm which his mother had
given him. Although he did not believe the Tulasi-beads
around his neck dispensed good fortune, he refused to take
off the necklace. Gandhi recalled a Quaker friend arguing:

> "This superstition does not become you. Come,
> let me break the necklace."
> "No, you will not," [Gandhi replied.] "It is a sacred
> gift from my mother."
> "But do you believe in it?"
> "I do not know its mysterious significance. I do
> not think I should come to harm if I did not wear it.

> But I cannot, without sufficient reason, give up a neck-
> lace that she put round my neck out of love and in
> the conviction that it would be conducive to my wel-
> fare. When, with the passage of time, it wears away
> and breaks of its own accord, I shall have no desire to
> get a new one. But this necklace cannot be broken."[12]

Herein lay Gandhi's core message: try to see the good rather
than the bad in other people, and in other people's beliefs. Of
religion, he wrote:

> It is no business of mine to criticise the scriptures of
> other faiths, or to point out their defects. It is and
> should be, however, my privilege to proclaim and
> practise the truths that there may be in them. I may
> not, therefore, criticise or condemn things in the Ko-
> ran or the life of the Prophet that I cannot under-
> stand. But I welcome every opportunity to express
> my admiration for such aspects of his life as I have
> been able to appreciate and understand.[13]

How alien is Gandhi's thinking to the modern world! The
twenty-first century has opened with a revival of inter-faith
condemnation, be it Christians denouncing Islam, Muslims
demonising Judaism, Catholics sneering at Protestantism, or
secularists — like Harris — lampooning all of the above.
Naturally, the followers of one faith should be free to comment on the beliefs of another. But tolerance decrees that
there is a right and a wrong way of so commenting.

Cardinal Joseph Ratzinger, the man who would become
Pope Benedict XVI, had been criticised in some quarters for
going about things the wrong way. Critics listed as diplomatic
indiscretions his description of Buddhist practices as "auto-

erotic",[14] his allusion to the warring Muslim stereotype when portraying Turkey as "in permanent contrast" to Europe,[15] and his dismissal of Protestant denominations as "not churches in the proper sense".[16] But how fair was it, or is it, to judge someone on a few isolated comments, especially such as those above, which were greatly qualified by either the Cardinal himself or his Congregation for the Doctrine of the Faith? Is it fair to describe him as intolerant when, unlike other religious leaders, he has at least tried to engage in a debate with people of other faiths?

The issue comes into sharper focus when one considers the response to a letter on "the Pastoral Care of Homosexual Persons", which was signed by Cardinal Ratzinger and sent to Catholic Bishops in 1986. The letter read:

> It is deplorable that homosexual persons have been and are the object of violent malice in speech or in action. . . . The intrinsic dignity of each person must always be respected in word, in action and in law. But the proper reaction to crimes committed against homosexual persons should not be to claim that the homosexual condition is not disordered. When such a claim is made and when homosexual activity is consequently condoned, or when civil legislation is introduced to protect behaviour to which no one has any conceivable right, neither the Church nor society at large should be surprised when other distorted notions and practices gain ground, and irrational and violent reactions increase.[17]

It is easy to see how people could take offence at such comments, as indeed many homosexuals did when they were published. The Cardinal reiterated the Church's view that gays and lesbians are to be pitied but not despised in a spirit of "loving the sinner but hating the sin". It is a patronising view (and one this author wholly disagrees with). But is the best answer to that view challenging the Cardinal's right to say what he said? After all, taking offence is a form of intolerance itself. It declares, in effect, that the comments in question breached the bounds of acceptability, and should be withdrawn and apologised for.

Here we alight upon an important dimension to tolerance, as intellectual modesty. The virtue entails not just moderation in speech but temperance in one's own expectation of others. It means hoping people will see the good in your opinions, your lifestyle or your faith but not demanding it. It means allowing people to accept you even if they don't "celebrate" you, or condone what you believe in. I for one would welcome the Pope celebrating the notion of loving homosexual relationships but it is unreasonable of me to take offence at his failing to do so.

That is not in any way to defend Cardinal Ratzinger's opinion on homosexuality but merely to emphasise that the intolerant are easily offended, Harris arguably being a case in point. While he condemns religion for using incendiary or deliberately divisive language, he himself describes religious belief as "mad", "psychotic" and "delusional", summarising the Eucharist in Catholicism as eating Jesus Christ "in the form of a cracker". His prose is undoubtedly punchy but the scientist, who confesses to be an admirer of eastern philosophy,[18] should perhaps take note of Gandhi's words: "cultivation of tolerance for other faiths will impart to us a truer understanding of our own."[19] There is no better way to avoid the flaws in one's own belief system than to attack those in others'.

Returning to the view of eastern faiths, Taoism — like Buddhism and Hinduism — identifies practical benefits in being tolerant. It regards as an undeniable truth the fact that human nature is diverse; thus, trying to eradicate diversity is futile.

> The duck's legs are short, but if we try to lengthen them, the duck will feel pain. The crane's legs are long, but if we try to shorten them, the crane will feel grief. Therefore we are not to amputate what is by nature long, nor to lengthen what is by nature short.[20]

So argued influential Taoist thinker Chuang Tzu. He said people should adhere to their individual nature rather than impose their nature on others. Even well-intentioned interference was to be avoided, as another of his anecdotes affirmed:

> Of old, when a seabird alighted outside the capital of Lu, the Marquis went out to receive it, gave it wine in the temple and had the Chiu-shao music played to it, and a bullock slaughtered to feed it. But the bird was dazed and too timid to eat or drink anything. In three days it was dead. This was treating the bird as one would treat oneself, not the bird as a bird.[21]

Such tolerance is undoubtedly linked to Taoism's positive, and some might say romantic, view of man's natural condition. Taoists maintain that man is born good, and is conditioned to perform evil acts by society. In this way, they counsel against invasive government, if not all government, claiming that people left to their own devices will be happy and at peace.

Traces of such idealistic thinking can be found in Confucianism, particularly in the teachings of Mencius who believed that people were born with *jen* — the supreme virtue of human-heartedness — but who, in their quest for social acceptance and material pleasure, forgot how to practise it. Mencius' view, however, was far from universally accepted in Confucianism. As we read in the chapter on loyalty, Hsun Tzu (c.310–237 BCE), another of Confucius' disciples, had a more sober opinion of man's essential character, arguing that the strong arm of the law was all that was holding society back from anarchy.

Firmer ground for tolerance in Confucianism can be found in *The Doctrine of the Mean*, which endorses a religious, and sometimes baffling, devotion to "the middle course". This devotion applies to both action and belief. As one author notes: "It is a Confucian tenet that healthy interaction of modern cultures of the East and West will eventually lead to the 'higher form of creative synthesis which will emerge as a new culture of the future with both the East and the West as its necessary ingredients'."[22]

Confucianism's pragmatic streak has been described as "non-prescriptivity", the principle that one person should not decide what is best for the next. The benefits of such thinking are hailed in Chinese folktales like the following, which blends a traditional cautionary theme with no small amount of Confucian chauvinism:

> A king threw a banquet for his ministers and generals. His daughter walked among the guests, filling their glasses. Suddenly, a gust of wind blew out the candles — at which point, the princess felt a man pull

at her clothes. She quickly fended off the assailant and in the process ripped the chin-ribbon off his hat. She immediately ran to the king and demanded punishment. But instead of exposing the culprit, he told all his guests "Let's not be formal. Let's all take off our hats and rip off the ribbons."

Some years later, the king's army was at war. Defeat was averted only thanks to the bravery of one of his generals whom the king immediately summoned to his court. When asked why he had fought so hard, the general explained that he had been the guest who had harassed the princess at the banquet all those years ago. "You generously overlooked my fault," the general continued. "From that day on, I've been seeking a chance to demonstrate my gratitude."

The king replied, "I am glad I did not listen to the princess."23

Tolerance, in this context, is closely aligned to mercy — a virtue to be dealt with in its own right in a later chapter. First, however, let's return to the question of how some faiths embrace tolerance less enthusiastically than others. Christianity provides no shortage of historical examples of intolerance, from the Inquisition and the Crusades of the Middle Ages to today's occasional — and some would argue growing — hostility towards Islam. Several evangelical ministers in the US have made names for themselves by criticising Muslim belief, describing Muhammad as "the antichrist" and "a demon-obsessed paedophile".24 Most famously, Franklin Graham, son of the famous Billy Graham, a close friend of the US President George W. Bush, described Islam as "very evil and wicked". But how representative are such people of Christianity? Or, for that matter, the President? (Bush himself has described Islam as a religion of peace, which "brings comfort to a billion people around the world".)

The official position of the Catholic Church since Vatican II is one of religious inclusivism, whereby one religion (Catholicism) is fully correct but other faiths participate in revealing some of the truth of that religion. More importantly, in terms of establishing the true meaning of Christianity, consider what Jesus had to say about tolerance:

> Do not judge others, so that God will not judge you, for God will judge you in the same way as you judge others, and he will apply to you the same rules you apply to others. Why, then, do you look at the speck in your brother's eye, and pay no attention to the log in your own eye? How dare you say to your brother, "Please, let me take that speck out of your eye," when you have a log in your own eye? You hypocrite! First take the log out of your own eye, and then you will be able to see clearly to take the speck out of your brother's eye.[25]

A pertinent example of Jesus' own tolerance can be found in Luke's Gospel:

> As the time drew near when Jesus would be taken up to heaven, he made up his mind and set out on his way to Jerusalem. He sent messengers ahead of him, who went into a village in Samaria to get everything ready for him. But the people there would not receive him, because it was clear that he was on his way to Jerusalem. When the disciples James and John saw this, they said, "Lord, do you want us to call fire down from heaven to destroy them?"

Jesus turned and rebuked them. Then Jesus and his
disciples went on to another village.[26]

Islam similarly warns against judging others, demanding tolerance, particularly for other "people of the Book", as Christians and Jews are known in the faith. As well as calling on
people to conduct their affairs by "mutual consultation",[27] the
Qur'an emphasises that "the reality of human diversity is part
of the divine wisdom, and an intentional purpose of creation".[28] It states:

Unto every one of you We have appointed a [differ-
ent] law and way of life. And if God had so willed He
could surely have made you all one single community:
but [He willed it otherwise] in order to test you by
means of what He has vouchsafed for you. Vie, then,
with one another in doing good works! Unto God
you all must return; and then He will make you understand all that on which you were wont to differ.[29]

Tolerance is further extolled in the sayings of Muhammad.
The following, recorded by al-Bukhari, the most esteemed
collector of *hadiths* in Islam, is particularly noteworthy:

Two persons, a Muslim and a Jew, quarrelled. The
Muslim said, "By Him Who gave Muhammad superiority over all the people!" The Jew said, "By Him Who
gave Moses superiority over all the people!" At that
the Muslim raised his hand and slapped the Jew on the
face. The Jew went to the Prophet and informed him
of what had happened between him and the Muslim.
The Prophet sent for the Muslim and asked him about
it. The Muslim informed him of the event. The
Prophet said, "Do not give me superiority over

Moses, for on the Day of Resurrection all the people will fall unconscious and I will be one of them, but I will be the first to gain consciousness, and will see Moses standing and holding the side of the Throne [of Allah]. I will not know whether [Moses] has also fallen unconscious and got up before me, or Allah has exempted him from that stroke."[30]

Admittedly, however, the Islamic requirement to be tolerant of "People of the Book" has been used by some conservative Muslims to justify intolerance towards the followers of eastern faiths, like Buddhism and Hinduism, as well as towards atheists. A typical expression of such intolerance can be found in the address of the influential Egyptian scholar Muhammad El-Ghazalli to the Parliament of the World's Religions, an unprecedented gathering of religious leaders, in Chicago in 1993. He said:

To consider the belief in God as a secondary, side issue, or an issue that is altogether unrelated to ethics, is something that is objectionable to us Muslims. In fact, it raises feelings of aversion and revolt. Why should God be the Creator and others be worshipped in His stead? Why should God be the Giver and Provider and others be thanked instead? Why should ingratitude be considered a vice except in our relationship with God? . . . I think that atheists should be disregarded in this respect, but if we have to sit with them, then a special policy must be laid down to harmonise between our religious faith and their rights in life. Who knows, maybe our congeniality will one day guide them to the right and true path.[31]

Separately, El-Ghazalli spoke of the pleasure Muslims had in meeting "followers of the heavenly religions" — religions that esteemed goodness and condemned folly. Together "we can promote virtue and combat vice", he added, suggesting secularists stood in opposition to this mission.

But by seeing only bad in secularists and secularism, El-Ghazalli is, ironically, locked into the same intolerant outlook as Harris, who sees no good in the religious, nor religion.[32] And, just as Harris has his supporters in the secular world, El-Ghazalli is representative of countless conservative Muslims who associate secularism in its entirety with the worst excesses of western culture, such as conspicuous consumption, and the vulgar lifestyles of the rich and famous. However, many moderate Muslims have acknowledged positive aspects to liberal, secular society, like its endorsement of human rights, including the right to religious freedom, and its underlying humanitarian ethic. Khaled Abou El Fadl, a US-based authority on Islamic law, gives voice to such moderates by urging Muslims to see the good in all faiths — religious and otherwise. He asserts:

> The measure of moral virtue on this earth is who is able to come closer to divinity through justice, and not who carries the correct religious or irreligious label. The measure in the Hereafter is a different matter, but it is a matter that is in the purview of God's exclusive jurisdiction. . . . Considering the enormous diversity of human beings, we have no choice but to take each contribution to a vision of goodness seriously, and to ask which of the proffered visions comes closer to attempting to fulfil the divine charge.[33]

So where does this leave Harris's theory? His assertion that "respect for other faiths . . . is not an attitude that God endorses" contradicts reported statements by Jesus and Muhammad, among others. Of some validity perhaps is Harris's argument that "intolerance is . . . intrinsic to every creed". But, if by "intolerance" he means an unwillingness to accept certain perceived evils, then surely this goes for secular as well as religious creeds? A theory of human rights, for instance, is nothing if not intolerant of human rights abuses.

The only way to avoid "intolerance" in this sense is by believing in nothing. This, however, cannot be a virtue, and nor can it equate to tolerance. One is only tolerant if one believes a particular thing and chooses not to impose that belief on another, despite his or her offending viewpoint.

Tolerance also requires taking rival positions seriously. Diverse traditions, or cultures, should not be lowered — or raised — to the same level under a "presumption of equal respect or worth". Such a presumption, as one Confucian scholar points out, "implicitly smacks of cultural arrogance":

> The idea of presumption of equal worth of all cultures seems to imply, from the point of view of the speaker, that the other culture in question is bizarre, though he or she must reserve judgement pending further study. While this sort of attitude seems to display a liberal's generous response to "the politics of recognition", for many members of the minority cultural groups, it is a demeaning response to the "politics of difference". What is wanted is an *acknowledgement* of one's cultural integrity, without prejudgment, not "a presumption of equal worth".[34]

This point should be borne in mind, particularly by secular thinkers who define themselves by their opposition to organised religion, regarding all faiths to be equally mad or bad. Whatever about the merits of such thinking, it cannot be described as tolerant.

A final word on tolerance: like any of the virtues we have examined to date, it is not a panacea for the world's problems, and nor should it be practised to the extreme. It is no virtue, in other words, to ignore one's values for the sake of popularity, or convenience. Nor is it a virtue to unthinkingly accept a communal ethic of the lowest common denominator. Extreme tolerance is a recipe for disaster, as the protagonist in the Arab tale of *The Man with Two Wives* illustrates:

> A man had two wives, called Hana and Bana. One was older than him, the other younger. Both competed for his attention. The younger wanted him to appear youthful so she plucked the grey hairs from his head. The older wanted him to share her elderly appearance so she plucked out the dark hairs. So it continued until the man was completely bald.[35]

One could argue that secular society is today at risk of "falling between Hana and Bana" — as the phrase goes — and losing something more precious than its appearance. A society that promotes no values, and, say, ignores human rights abuses, condemns large sections of the population to poverty, or allows terrorism to go unpunished, is in terminal decline. And those who argue we should be tolerant of either injustice or tyranny are contributing to that fall, forgetting that a valueless world cannot be a tolerant one.

Endnotes

[1] Celaladin Rumi as quoted in Leeming, D. (2002), *Myth: A Biography of Belief*, Oxford University Press, pp. 6–7.

[2] UN Declaration of Human Rights (1948), Articles 18–19.

[3] Harris, S. (2005), *The End of Faith*, London: The Free Press, p. 46.

[4] Harris, S., *op. cit.*, p. 13.

[5] Ram-Prasad, C. (2001), "Multiplism: A Jaina Ethics of Toleration for a Complex World", in J. Runzo and N.M. Martin (eds.), *Ethics in the World Religions*, Oxford: Oneworld, p. 349–50.

[6] Ram-Prasad, C., *op. cit*, p. 353.

[7] Orwell, G. (1948), *Nineteen Eighty-Four*, London: Penguin, p. 223.

[8] Ram-Prasad, C., *op. cit.*, p. 360.

[9] Gandhi, M.K. (1946), *Hind Swaraj* (Indian Home Rule), Ahmedabad: Navajvan, p. 36.

[10] *Harjan*, 30 January 1937.

[11] Rumi, Jalal ad-Din, *Rubai of Mevlana*.

[12] Gandhi, M.K. (1927), *An Autobiography*, Ahmedabad, India: Navajivan Trust, p. 103.

[13] *Harjan*, 14 May 1938.

[14] The comments were made in an interview with a French newspaper, and subsequently translated into English. Some argue that what Ratzinger meant by "auto-eroticism" was really "self-absorption" or "narcissism". The Cardinal was separately accused of describing the Hindu concept of karma as "morally cruel".

[15] In an interview with France's *Le Figaro*, August 2004, Ratzinger said: "Throughout history Turkey has always represented another continent, in permanent contrast with Europe. There were the wars against the Byzantine Empire, the fall of Constantinople, the Balkan wars, and the threat against Vienna and Austria. That is why I think it would be an error to equate the two continents . . ."

[16] Congregation for the Doctrine of the Faith, *Dominus Iesus* (Lord Jesus), 6 August 2000, par 17.

[17] Congregation for the Doctrine of the Faith, "Letter to the Bishops of the Catholic Church on the Pastoral Care of Homosexual Persons", 1 October 1986, par. 10.

[18] Harris, S. op. cit. p. 204–21.

[19] *Young India* (Bulletin), 2 October 1930.

[20] Fung Yu-Lan (1948), *A Short History of Chinese Philosophy*, New York: The Free Press, pp. 105–6.

[21] Fung Yu-Lan, *op. cit.*, pp. 10–16.

[22] Cua A.S. (1998), *Moral Vision and Tradition*, Catholic University of America Press: Washington DC, p. 323.

[23] Adapted from Tang, C. (1996), *A Treasury of China's Wisdom*, Beijing: Foreign Languages Press, p. 189–90.

[24] Jerry Vines, former head of the Southern Baptist Convention, described Mohammed as a "demon-obsessed paedophile"; John Hanna, an evangelical minister from Ohio, claimed "the Muslim religion is an antichrist religion".

[25] Matthew 7:1–5.

[26] Luke 9:51–56.

[27] Qur'an 42:38.

[28] Qur'an 11:119 as quoted by Abou El-Fadl, K. (2003), "The Human Rights Commitment in Modern Islam" in J. Runzo, N.M. Martin and A. Sharma (eds.), *Human Rights and Responsibilities in the World Religions*, Oxford: Oneworld, p. 329.

[29] Qur'an 5:48.

[30] Hadith of al-Bukhari, Vol. 3, Book, No. 594.

[31] Kung, H. (eds.) (1995), *Yes to a Global Ethic*, London: SCM Press, pp. 182–3.

[32] Sheikh Muhammad El-Ghazalli (1917–1996), of Al-Azhar University in Cairo, was a prominent member of the Muslim Brotherhood, the radical Islamist group opposed to the secularisation of Arab states.

[33] Abou El-Fadl, K., *op. cit.*, p. 339.

[34] Cua A.S., *op. cit.*, p. 328.

[35] Other versions of this story can be found in Buckhardt, J.L. (1984), *Arabic Proverbs*, London: Curzon Press, p. 46–7; and Rhys, E. (eds.) (1928), *Aesop's Fables*, London: J.M. Dent & Sons, pp. 78–9.

10

WISDOM

One morning, a beggar approached a restaurant in the town where Nasrudin the Mullah lived. As he passed the premises by, the poor man stopped and sniffed, taking in the scent of the food being cooked inside. Suddenly, he heard a voice shout: "Come back here!"

It was the owner, storming out onto the street.

"You smelt my food without paying for it!"

As he had no money, the poor man was brought before the town *qadi* who said he would give his judgement the following day.

When morning came the beggar made his way to the *qadi's* court, expecting the worst. As he passed the mosque, however, he spotted Nasrudin whom he knew to be a wise man. The beggar explained his predicament, and Nasrudin agreed to come to court and speak on his behalf.

When they arrived, they saw the restaurant owner chatting with the *qadi*. It turned out they were friends, and the beggar's heart sunk. Sure enough, the *qadi* began to heap insults on the poor man, and ordered him to pay a large sum of money.

Suddenly, Nasrudin stepped forward, and offered to pay in his place.

The mullah took a bag of coins from his belt and held it next to the rich man's ear. He shook the bag so that the coins jingled.

"Do you hear that?" asked Nasrudin.

"Of course," the man replied impatiently.

"That is your payment," said the mullah. "My brother has smelled your food, and you have heard his money."

In the face of such argument, the case was settled and the poor man set free.[1]

Wisdom, as a religious virtue, should not be confused with cleverness. While the former is universally celebrated by the world's great faiths, the latter is treated with at best indifference, and at worst hostility. There is no special praise for intelligence in the Qur'an; no "Blessed are the brainy" in the Bible. In some philosophies, cleverness is a hallmark of arrogance and, as such, should be avoided. Socrates, who retains an influence over both religious and secular thinking in the west, railed against conventional education, advocating "unlearning" instead. "If there is one thing of which I am certain," he proudly declared, "it is that I know nothing." Lao Tzu, the father of Taoism, similarly boasted, "Mine is the mind of the very ignorant", while his disciple Chuang Tzu advocated *wang*, or forgetting, as a means to enlightenment. As for Islam, Ali, the Prophet Muhammad's cousin, reportedly said: "Whoever gives up saying 'I don't know' has been mortally stricken."[2]

Of all the world's faiths, Confucianism perhaps comes closest to endorsing education. Mother Meng, the tradition's matriarch, was said to have insisted on living next to a school so that her son, Mencius, would imitate the etiquette of the scholars. In essence, however, education, or knowledge, in itself is morally neutral in Confucianism — as it tends to be in other religions. What matters to the world's major faiths is how you put your knowledge to use. "He who learns but does not think is lost," said Confucius. "He who thinks but does not learn is in danger."[3] It is the good effect to which Nasrudin's knowledge had been put which makes the opening story a tale of wisdom rather than cleverness.

Yet the wisdom of Nasrudin is just one form of the virtue, which is also understood by the world's major faiths as a type of "meta-virtue" which provides guidance to other character traits. In Buddhism, for instance, wisdom is listed as one of the six perfections, or *mahayana* virtues, of a bodhisattva. At the same time, Buddhist nirvana is described as a fusion of virtue and wisdom — the latter operating in this particular context as a moderating or harmonising influence on the human character. As for Confucianism, "wisdom" is the name given to the narrower — more earthly — virtue of applying knowledge well, while "learning" alludes to a superior, overarching trait. As Confucius put it:

> One who loves humanity but not learning will be obscured by ignorance. One who loves wisdom but not learning will be obscured by lack of principle. One who loves faithfulness but not learning will be obscured by heartlessness. One who loves uprightness but not learning will be obscured by violence. One

who loves strength of character but not learning will
be obscured by recklessness.[4]

Learning, or wisdom in this broader sense, implies a harmony
of words and deeds, or "the unity of knowledge and action",
to use a famous saying of the neo-Confucian Wang Yang-Ming
(1472–1527).[5] Confucianism, thus, draws upon the Socratean
principle that it is impossible to perform an action that you
know deep down to be wrong. Buddhism concurs, arguing,
for example, that sadism arises from ignorance because it
means treating another person as a non-person in defiance of
the actuality.

In Hinduism, wisdom is similarly synonymous with goodness. The intersection between the two concepts is dramati-
cally encapsulated in the epic *Mahabharata*, which centres on
the adventures of Yudhishthira. As the righteous sage approaches heaven's gate, he encounters the god Dharma who,
disguised as "The Voice", tests Yudhishthira on all things
worth knowing. Here is a flavour of the dialogue:

> The Voice said: "Who makes the sun rise? Who
> keeps him company? Who makes the sun go down? In
> whom is the sun established?"
> Said Yudhishthira: "Brahma makes the sun rise; the
> gods accompany him; Dharma makes the sun to set;
> in truth is the sun established."
> The Voice said: "What sleeps with open eyes?
> What moves not after birth? What has no heart?
> What swells of itself?"
> Said Yudhishthira: "A fish sleeps with open eyes;
> an egg moves not after birth; a stone has no heart; a
> river swells of itself" . . .

> The Voice said: "Who is the unconquered enemy
> of man? What is the enemy's disease? Who is holy?
> Who is unholy?"
>
> Said Yudhishthira: "Man's unconquered enemy is
> anger, and his disease is covetousness; he who seeks
> after the good of all is holy; he who is selfishly cold is
> unholy."
>
> The Voice said: "Who are worthy of eternal tor-
> ment?"
>
> Said Yudhishthira: "He who says to a Brahman in-
> vited to his house, I have naught to give; he who de-
> clares the Vedas to be false; he who is rich and yet
> gives nothing to the poor."[6]

What makes Yudhishthira wise, of course, is that he not only
talks the talk but walks the walk. He knows what it is to be
virtuous and, in the *Mahabharata,* applies that knowledge
without fail.

But, by so closely aligning wisdom with goodness, do the
world's faiths kill off the virtue, as understood in the narrower
sense of a healthy mental quality exemplified, for instance, in
Nasrudin's quick-wittedness? Not necessarily: wisdom retains
an identity of its own — as a virtue that draws together such
traits as simplicity and calmness of mind, an ability to admit to
one's errors and a sense of perspective. The first of these
three qualities is particularly associated with Chinese religion.
Recall Confucius' words: "The man who is simple and slow to
speak is near to humanity."[7] To this, Chuang Tzu added: "The
mind of the perfect man is like a mirror. It does not move with
things, nor does it anticipate them. It responds to things but is
not affected by them."[8] Almost 2,000 years later, the European
philosopher Benedict de Spinoza made a similar point when he

wrote "the ignorant man is . . . agitated by external causes", while "the wise man . . . is scarcely moved in his mind".[9]

Both calmness and simplicity of thought are also celebrated in Christianity, the former perhaps most famously in the "serenity prayer" — a prayer commonly attributed to the Protestant theologian Reinhold Niebuhr:

> God, grant me the serenity to accept the things I cannot change, the courage to change the things I can, and the wisdom to know the difference.

Simplicity is meanwhile endorsed by Bible stories in which "ordinary folk" are portrayed as wiser than the supposedly learned scribes and Pharisees. A common criticism of the Catholic Church down the ages is that it has embraced complexity in defiance of Jesus' teachings, and St Francis of Assisi, for one, called for a return to *simplicitas* as a guiding principle for Christians. It was perhaps heartening in this regard that Pope Benedict XVI — a man accused of hiding behind complicated dogma as a cardinal — declared in his inaugural sermon in April 2005: "To everyone I turn with simplicity and with affection, in the assurance that the church wants to construct an open and sincere dialogue in the search for true good for man and society."[10]

What of the other hallmarks of wisdom: an ability to admit to one's errors and a sense of perspective? They are well illustrated in a tale from the *Jakaka Stories*, in which the Buddha, or "Exalted One" encounters a number of "sectarians, recluses and brahmanas" arguing over the meaning of life:

> Now some of these recluses and brahmanas held such views as these: "Eternal is the world: this is the

truth, all else is delusion." Others held: "Not Eternal is the world: this is the truth, all else is delusion." Others again held: "The world is finite", or "The world is infinite". Or again: "Body and soul are one and the same." Others said: "Body and soul are different things.". . . And each maintained that his own view was the truth, and that all else was delusion.

So they lived quarrelsome, noisy, disputatious, abusing each other with words that pierced like javelins, maintaining: "This is the truth, that is not the truth. That is not the truth, this is the truth!" . . .

The Buddha settled the argument by telling a story of the blind men of Savatthi who were once gathered together and shown an elephant. One man was presented the head of elephant, the next the ear, the next a tusk, the next the trunk, the next a foot, the next the tail, and so on. Afterwards, the men were asked to describe an elephant. "An elephant is just like a pot," said the man who had been presented the head. "No, no, it's like a window basket," said the man who had observed the ear. "No, a ploughshare," said the man who got the tusk. "A plough," said the man with the trunk; "a pillar," the man with the foot; "a brush," the man with the tail. So they quarrelled until they came to blows about the matter. The "Exalted One" finished the story with this "solemn saying":

> O how they cling and wrangle, some who claim
> Of brahman and recluse the honoured name!
> For quarrelling, each to his view, they cling.
> Such folk see only one side of a thing.[11]

Other faiths similarly condemn narrow-mindedness. In the Judaeo-Christian tradition, wisdom is all about appreciating context. A classic tribute to the virtue can be found in Kohelet (Ecclesiastes):

> For Everything there is a season, and a time for every matter under heaven:
> A time to be born, and a time to die;
> A time to plant, and a time to pluck up what is planted;
> A time to kill, and a time to heal;
> A time to break down, and a time to build up;
> A time to weep, and a time to laugh;
> A time to mourn, and a time to dance;
> A time to throw away stones, and a time to gather stones together;
> A time to embrace, and a time to refrain from embracing;
> A time to seek, and a time to lose,
> A time to keep, and a time to throw away;
> A time to tear, and a time to sew;
> A time to keep silence, and a time to speak;
> A time to love, and a time to hate;
> A time for war, and a time for peace.[12]

To better understand wisdom, however, examine how the world's great faiths answer a practical question: for example, how should one deal with misfortune? The question is of deep concern to all faiths and, in Buddhism, the answer comes in a parable.

> There once was a woman called Kisagotami, who lost her only son to illness when he was just a year old. Kisagotami was broken-hearted, and in her grief, went from door to door, asking for medicine that would bring her son back to life. Eventually, she arrived at the house of the Buddha who felt sorry for her.

"I will help you," the Buddha said. "But first you must bring me a mustard seed from a house where no one has died."

Kisagotami hurried into the town and stopped at the first house she saw. "I need a mustard seed," she said. "From a house where no one has died."

"I'm sorry," the reply came. "You can have a mustard seed with pleasure. But our grandmother died last year."

And so Kisagotami went to the next house. But there she was told: "I'm sorry but our brother died not so long ago."

Everywhere she went, the answer was the same. People wanted to help but they could not. In every house she visited, someone had died. And then she understood. She took her son to be buried, and then returned to the Buddha.

"Have you got the mustard seed?" the Buddha asked. "No," Kisagotami replied. "But now I see that I am not alone in my sorrow. Everything changes; it is part of life. And death must come to everyone sooner or later."[13]

In Chinese philosophy, the question of misfortune is also addressed in a parable:

A long time ago, in a remote Chinese province, there was a farmer whose horse ran away. His neighbours came to express their sympathy. But the farmer asked: "How do you know it isn't a blessing?"

Some time later, the horse returned with a herd of wild horses. Friends and neighbours gathered to admire the animals and congratulate the farmer. But he asked: "How do you know it isn't a curse?"

> After a while, the farmer got his son to help him
> train the wild horses. But one day the youngster fell
> off and broke his leg. Everyone came to console him.
> However, the farmer replied: "Good luck? Bad Luck?
> Who knows?"
>
> Weeks later, the nomads invaded China and every
> horseman in the province was conscripted. But, be-
> cause of his broken leg, the farmer's son was ex-
> empted from duty.
>
> As legend has it, the Chinese army lost nine of out
> every ten men in the border conflict.[14]

Taken together, the two stories suggest that, in a moral sense,
knowledge and the lack of it are two sides of the same coin.
Kisagotami was wise because she appreciated that humans
were mortal. The farmer was wise because he realised that he
hadn't any of the answers. Her "knowledge" and his "ignorance" were identical in that they produce the same mental
approach — an approach fittingly called "philosophical", as it
was pioneered by the father of western philosophy, Socrates.
As he faced execution, the sage of Athens was calmness personified, reasoning:

> If you see anyone distressed at the prospect of dying,
> it will be proof enough that he is a lover not of wis-
> dom but of the body. As a matter of fact, I suppose
> he is also a lover of wealth and reputation; one or the
> other, or both.[15]

Once Socrates had taken the poison that would claim his life,
his friends broke down in tears. The philosopher was unim-
pressed:

Really, my friends, what a way to behave! Why, that
was my main reason for sending away the women, to
prevent this sort of disturbance.[16]

Wisdom, in this context, could be translated as equanimity,
or evenness of temper in the face of good fortune, or ill.
Nothing is as unwise, sages from the Buddha to Socrates declare, than to treat one's current predicament as somehow
permanent. The lesson is reinforced in stories of the "don't
count your chickens before they have hatched" variety. This
tale, typical of the genre, comes from Buddhist lore:

There was once a Brahman, Devasharman by
name, in the town of Devakotta. One day someone
gave him a present of a pot of barley, so, taking it
with him, he went to a potter's shed which was filled
with pots of every size; there he lay down and there
he began to ponder during the night:

"If I were to sell this pot of barley I would get ten
gold pieces; with that money I could buy pitchers and
pots. These I could sell at a profit and, with my
money increased, I could trade in *betel* nut, silks and
the like, so that soon I would be worth thousands.
This way I could marry four wives, and of course I
would especially favour the most beautiful among the
four. Then, if the co-wives began to quarrel with her
out of jealousy, I would get angry and beat them with
a stick like this!"

Hereupon he lashed out with a stick he was holding in his hand. As a result, not only was his own pot
of barley smashed, but many other pots as well.

When the potter, who had been roused by the
sound of the pots being smashed, saw what had happened, he swore at the Brahman and drove him out

of his shed. Truly it is said that he who rejoices about things which have not yet happened is likely to suffer great scorn.[17]

Is it always wise to be equanimous, however? If one is faced with an injustice, or a personal challenge in one's life, surely the right response is a determined refusal to accept things as they are rather than a mere sigh of resignation. Equanimity practised to the extreme seems to be a recipe for docility. Here, we return to the notion of wisdom in the broader sense, as a harmonising virtue governing all others. The truly wise are never one-dimensional. They are equanimous in one instance, and just in another. They are loyal in one set of circumstances and audacious in the next, reflecting the fact that they know, among other things, when and how to practise each particular virtue.

The best portraits of wisdom are, thus, epics rather than stand-alone tales. The *Mahabharata* gives us one description of the virtue, the story of Solomon another.

Whatever about his importance as an historical figure, Solomon has a profound religious significance as he crops up not only in Jewish and Christian literature but also in Islamic lore (where he is known as Sulaiman or Suleiman). One Muslim tale recalls the future prophet attending, as a young boy, the court of his father, David. Solomon was only eleven years old but already somewhat gifted. The story goes:

> One day, David was sitting as usual solving the problems of his people when two men, one of whom had a field, came to him. The owner of the field said: "O dear Prophet! This man's sheep came to my field at night and ate up the grapes and I have come to ask

for compensation." David asked the owner of the sheep: "Is this true?" He said: "Yes sir!" David said: "I have decided that you give him your sheep in exchange for the field." Solomon, whom Allah had given wisdom in addition to what he inherited from his father, spoke up: "I have another option. The owner of the sheep should take the field to cultivate until the grapes grow. While the other man should take the sheep and make use of their wool and milk till his field is fixed. If the grapes grow and the field returns to its former state, then the [field-owner] should take his field and give back the sheep to their owner." David responded: "This is a sound judgement, praise be to Allah for gifting you with wisdom. You are truly Solomon the Wise."[18]

The wisdom of Solomon, as depicted in religious literature, may seem somewhat unobtainable to the average reader. After all, this was a character who, according to Islamic legend, could speak to animals and deploy the services of jinn in the management of his affairs. However, in Islam as in other traditions, Solomon was not the perfect human being. There is no contradiction in this fact because wisdom is not perfection. It is rather an ability to recognise and learn from one's imperfections. The lesson is reaffirmed in a final tale — this one from Jewish folklore — which also asserts the traditional religious viewpoint that everything worth knowing can be summed up in a few words:

> King Solomon had all the wealth and prestige a man could hope for. Yet he was often depressed. He dreamt one night that there existed a ring which con-

tained the knowledge that would bring him peace of mind, and so he sent his advisors out in search of it.

Six months later, the advisors returned empty-handed — all, that is, but one. The youngest servant had procured a ring from an aged street vendor to whom he had explained the king's predicament. It was a plain gold ring with a simple engraving on it.

Solomon looked at the ring and read the Hebrew words engraved there: *Gam Zeh Ya'avor* — "This too, shall pass". As he read, the king's sorrows turned to joy, and his joys to sorrow, and then both gave way to peace. The king was reminded in that moment that all his riches and glory were impermanent, and all his sorrows would pass away as the seasons and the years.

From that time on, King Solomon wore the ring and was reminded, in good times and bad, that "This too, shall pass."[19]

Endnotes

[1] Adapted from Khattab, H. (1987), *Stories from the Muslim World*, London: Macdonald, pp. 40–1.

[2] Cleary, T. (translator) (1997), *Living A Good Life: Advice on Virtue, Love, and Action from the Ancient Greek Masters*, Boston & London: Shambhala, p. 100.

[3] *The Analects*: 2:15.

[4] *The Analects* 17:8.

[5] Cua A.S. (1998), *Moral Vision and Tradition*, Catholic University of America Press: Washington DC, p. 271.

[6] Mackenzie D.A. (1913), *Indian Myth and Legend*, London: Gresham Publishing, pp. 264–7.

[7] *The Analects* 13:27.

[8] Chuang-Tzu, Ch. 7.

[9] *Ethics*, Pt. 5, Prop. XLII.

[10] *The Irish Times*, 21 April 2005.

11 Woodward, F.L. (1925), *Buddhist Stories*, Madras, India: Theosophical Publishing House, pp. 22–6.

12 Ecclesiastes 3:1–8.

13 Adapted form Ganeri, A. (2001), *Buddhist Stories*, London: Evans, p. 22–3. For an Arabic version of the story see Bushnaq, I. (1986), *Arab Folktales*, London & New York: Penguin Books, pp. 44–5.

14 Adapted from De Mello, A. (1978), *Sadhana: A Way to God*, Illinois: Doubleday, p. 140.

15 *Phaedo*, 68B.

16 *Phaedo*, 117A–118.

17 Gray J.E.B. (1961), *Indian Tales and Legends*, Oxford University Press, p. 212.

18 Bahgat, A. (1997), *Stories of the Prophets*, Cairo: Islamic Home Publishing & Distribution, pp. 317–18.

19 Talmudic story in Davy Pearmain, E. (1998), *Doorways to the Soul*, Cleveland, Ohio: The Pilgrim Press, pp. 21-1.

11

WORK

The little red hen found a grain of wheat. "Who will plant this?" she asked. "Not I," said the cat. "Not I," said the duck. "Then I will do it myself," said the little red hen, and she buried the wheat in the ground.

After a while the wheat began to ripen. "Who will cut and thresh it?" asked the little red hen. "Not I," said the cat. "Not I," said the duck. "Then I will do it myself," said the little red hen, and she cut the wheat with her beak and threshed it with her wings.

Then she asked, "Who will take this wheat to the mill?" "Not I," said the cat. "Not I," said the duck. "Then I will," said little red hen, and she took the wheat to the mill where she ground it into flour.

She carried the flour home and then asked: "Who will make some bread from this flour?" "Not I," said the cat. "Not I," said the duck. "Then I will," said the little red hen.

She made and baked the bread, and then asked: "Now who will eat this bread?" "We will," the cat and

> duck replied in unison. "No you won't," said the little
> red hen. "I'll do it myself." And she ate the bread up
> without any help at all.

That work is regarded far and wide as a virtue is undeniable.
The question is, why? What makes graft good? The nursery
story above has been passed down from generation to generation purportedly with a lesson for us all. But what is it that
is so commendable about the actions of the little red hen?

For some answers, at least from a Catholic perspective,
consider *Laborem Exercens*, the Encyclical Letter of Pope John
Paul II on "human work". In labouring, the Pope argued, man
was obeying God's order, as stated in Genesis, namely, "Fill
the earth and subdue it." According to the Pontiff, the Book
of Genesis not only confirmed that God was "the Creator"
but "it teaches that man ought to imitate God, his Creator, in
working, because man alone has the unique characteristic of
likeness to God".[1] And what an example to follow! God created the universe, not in seven years, nor seven months but
seven days (or strictly six, if one excludes the Sabbath). The
Creator is industriousness personified. On a more human
level, both Old and New Testaments contain many references to the value of occupations, from medicine to sailing.
Pope John Paul described the teachings of St Paul as "particularly lively" on the subject.

> Paul boasts of working at his trade (he was probably a
> tent-maker), and thanks to that work he was able even
> as an Apostle to earn his own bread. "With toil and la-
> bour we worked night and day, that we might not bur-
> den any of you." Hence his instructions, in the form of
> *exhortation and command*, on the subject of work:

"Now such persons we command and exhort in the
Lord Jesus Christ to do their work in quietness and to
earn their own living," he writes to the Thessalonians.
In fact, noting that some "are living in idleness . . . not
doing any work", the Apostle does not hesitate to say
in the same context: "If any one will not work, let him
not eat." In another passage he encourages his readers:
"Whatever your task, work heartily, as serving the
Lord and not men, knowing that from the Lord you
will receive the inheritance as your reward."[2]

From a Christian perspective, however, the most important
endorsement of work comes not from Paul but from Jesus
who "devoted most of the years of his life on earth to *manual
work* at the carpenter's bench". Jesus gave up the occupation
only to concentrate on his "work of salvation". In both tasks,
he displayed what the Pope called the "virtue of industriousness", a virtue manifested in perseverance, toil and suffering.
Jesus himself emphasised this labouring aspect of his mission
by describing himself as a "shepherd", and his disciples as
"fishers of men". Pope John Paul concluded on the subject:

The Christian finds in human work a small part of the
Cross of Christ and accepts it in the same spirit of redemption in which Christ accepted his Cross for us.[3]

Jesus is by no means alone among religious icons in displaying
a strong work-ethic. The Buddha endured all kinds of hard-
ships in his quest for enlightenment. Both he and Confucius
also worked as political advisors to the rulers of their day.
The latter may have been without paid employment on occasion but he was never idle. Indeed, Confucius developed the
reputation of a workaholic, using his spare time to practise

music, perfect his archery skills, and concentrate on studies. Moreover, he preached what he practised, declaring:

> When there is anything not yet studied, or studied but not yet understood, do not give up. When there is any question not yet asked, or asked but its answer not yet known, do not give up. When there is anything not yet thought over, or thought over but not yet apprehended, do not give up. When there is anything not yet sifted, or sifted but not yet clear, do not give up. When there is anything not yet practised, or practised but not yet earnestly, do not give up. If another man succeed by one effort, you will use a hundred efforts. If another man succeed by ten efforts, you will use a thousand efforts.[4]

A shared assertion of Confucianism and Buddhism is that to achieve anything worthwhile one must expend some effort. Neither moral nor material success is possible without toil. "Sow an act, reap a habit; sow a habit, reap a character; sow a character, reap a destiny," runs one Anglo-Buddhist proverb.[5] Neo-Confucians speak of practice, not just making perfect but, *being perfection*. A particular hallmark of the superior man in Confucianism is the power of concentration. A popular Chinese tale recalls how Mencius once returned home early from school when he was still a young pupil:

> "Why did you come back so early today?" Mother Meng asked, still weaving at her loom.
> "I miss you, mother."
> Without a word, Mother Meng took out a knife and cut the yarn on the loom right in the middle. Mencius was startled.

"For you to suspend your study at school is just like for me to cut the yarn on my loom. We are poor. That is why I've been working so hard. You have to study hard to establish yourself. If you do not concentrate on your studies and stop halfway, we will never be able to break the bondage of poverty. We will always have to lead a precarious life."

From then on, Mencius devoted himself completely to learning.[6]

Like many other morality tales, the story raises a question about motivation. Does Mencius embrace work simply because it will bring him material reward, and, if so, is his working virtuous? To be consistent with other virtues, work is surely virtuous only if it is performed without an earthly goal in mind.

The world's religious traditions are somewhat ambiguous on the matter. While they purport to celebrate industriousness for its own sake, they often preach a somewhat political — and perhaps politically conservative — sermon, stressing that toil brings success and laziness failure. In one Chinese folktale, a famous adviser to the prime minister of Qi visits the province and is horrified by the poverty around him. His solution is to cut back all the trees on the roads. The story continues:

Within a year, the life of those people visibly improved. They wore better clothes and had new shoes.

[The adviser explained:] "The trees offered a shade on the roadway. . . . Before they were trimmed, men and women in the neighbourhood often gathered there in the shade gossiping and playing games. . . . Some young people took to shooting birds in the trees. But they should have been working. Now the trees have

been trimmed. They no longer have the shade to avoid
the hot sun. No more dilly-dallying for them. They
have to work and make money. Naturally they are better off than before."[7]

Islam is particularly intolerant of laziness in society. Built into
the faith's notion of mutual responsibility is the idea that no-
body should unnecessary drain their neighbours' resources.
The wealthy should help the poor but the poor, in turn, should
try to escape the need for help. According to one *hadith*, Muhammad barred "the rich and able-bodied" from seeking charity. "It is better that a person should take a rope and bring a
bundle of wood on his back to sell so that Allah may preserve
his honour, than that he should beg from people . . ."[8]

There is a strong utilitarian streak to such thinking. In fact,
few sins are as maligned in Muslim literature as uselessness.
The Islamic "rationalist" and philosopher 'Abd al-Jabbar wrote
extensively on the subject, confirming "injury may be evil because it is useless, even though it is not wrong". Among the
examples he gave of "evil caused by uselessness" were:

> A man allows another to beat him, on condition that
> the beater compensates him with something more ad-
> vantageous to him than not being beaten. The agreed
> acts are carried out, no wrong has been done, yet the
> beating is evil. Why? Because it is useless. . . . A drown-
> ing man allows another to pull him out of the sea by his
> [the rescuer's] broken hand, and compensates him for
> that. There is no wrong done, since the compensation
> far exceeds the momentary pain, but the act is evil be-
> cause it could just as well have been performed by the
> rescuer using his sound hand. . . . A man hires another
> to pour water to no purpose from one part of the sea

to another. No harm is done to anyone, but it is evil as
[it is] useless. . . ."9

The last example raises a question about the quality of work
that people should perform, and whether some forms of employment are better than others. Before addressing that
question, however, consider how idleness is regarded outside
of Islam, and indeed outside of the context of the strictly religious. In his *Discourse on the Moral Effects of the Arts and Sciences*, Jean-Jacques Rousseau argued that "to live without
doing some good is a great evil in the political as in the moral
world; and hence every useless citizen should be regarded as
a pernicious person."10

Max Weber, the sociologist and enthusiast of the "Protestant work-ethic", described "waste of time" as "the first
and in principle the deadliest of sins". He wrote:

> The span of human life is infinitely short and precious
> to make sure of one's own election. Loss of time
> through sociability, idle talk, luxury, even more sleep
> than is necessary for health . . . is worthy of absolute
> moral condemnation . . .11

Even more damning of sloth was Leo Tolstoy who spoke of
man's tendency to "stupefy himself" rather than persevere in
work of value. He said:

> In any labour, especially at the beginning, there comes
> a time when the work seems painfully difficult, and
> our human weakness prompts us to abandon it.
> Physical labour seems painful at the beginning; intel-
> lectual labour all the more so. As [the German phi-
> losopher Gotthold Ephraim] Lessing says, people have
> a tendency to stop thinking when it first becomes

difficult; and it is at that point, I would add, that thinking becomes fruitful.[12]

By stupefying himself — through alcohol consumption and
other distractions (Tolstoy wrote before the days of television) — man could avoid the "painful labour" of trying to resolve the fundamental questions of existence. Tolstoy
continued:

> It is almost as though a man who wanted to see to the
> bottom of some muddy water in order to lay his hands
> on a precious pearl, but who wanted not to have to
> enter the water, were to stir up the water on purpose
> as soon as it began to settle and clear. Often a man
> stupefies himself all through his life, staying with the
> same obscure, self-contradictory view of the world to
> which he is accustomed, pushing at every moment of
> dawning clarity against the same wall as he did ten or
> twenty years before, unable to break through the wall
> because he has consciously blunted the blade of
> thought which alone could penetrate it.[13]

Laziness has had its defenders, among them the author
Robert Louis Stevenson who described "extreme business"
as "a symptom of deficient vitality". He wrote:

> Look at one of your industrious fellows for a mo-
> ment, I beseech you. He sows hurry and reaps indi-
> gestion; he puts a vast deal of activity out to interest,
> and receives a large measure of nervous derangement
> in return. Either he absents himself entirely from all
> fellowship, and lives a recluse in a garret, with carpet
> slippers and a leaden inkpot; or he comes among
> people swiftly and bitterly, in a contraction of his
> whole nervous system, to discharge some temper

before he returns to work. I do not care how much
or how well he works, this fellow is an evil feature in
other people's lives. They would be happier if he
were dead.[14]

Stevenson's *Apology for Idlers*, however, was not so much a
condemnation of work as of its unthinking glorification — a
glorification he witnessed at first hand in his own Scots Pres-
byterian upbringing. "It is certain," he admitted, "that much
may be judiciously argued in favour of diligence."

Lao Tzu, a contemporary of the Confucius, may similarly
have been reacting against the workaholic lifestyles of his
peers when he wrote in defence of inactivity: "Do nothing,
and there is nothing that is not done."[15]

To illustrate the point, the "father" of Taoism told a story
of a sacred oak which had been spared the axe because its
wood was good for nothing. The tree explained in a dream:

> For a long time I have been learning to be useless.
> There were several occasions on which I was nearly
> destroyed, but now I have succeeded in being useless,
> which is of the greatest use to me. If I were useful,
> could I have become so great?[16]

While other faiths may not be so enthusiastic about idleness,
they do warn against over-working. In his encyclical on human labour, Pope John Paul II said: "Man ought to imitate
God both in working and also in resting", particularly in resting every "seventh day".[17] Orthodox Christian teaching decrees that work is forbidden on the Sabbath, a day on which
church worship is in turn compulsory. Judaism is more prescriptive about its Shabbat — which lasts from dusk on Friday
to nightfall on Saturday — prohibiting 39 specific acts during

that time, including "hitting with a hammer", writing two let-
ters, and ploughing. The Neo-Confucian Wang Yang-Ming
also saw the need for rest, arguing: "If during the day one
feels work becoming annoying, one should sit in meditation.
But if one feels lazy and not inclined to read, then he should
go ahead and read. To do this is like applying medicine according to the disease."[18]

A common theme in all faiths is the need to combine intellectual and physical labour. According to the Jewish Mishnah:

> An excellent thing is the study of Torah combined with
> some worldly occupation, for the labour demanded by
> both of them causes sinful inclinations to be forgotten.
> All study of Torah without work must, in the end, be
> futile and become the cause of sin.[19]

The early Rabbis took this instruction to heart, earning their
livelihoods through a manual labour or trade. It is recorded:

> A favourite saying of the rabbis of Yavneh was: I am
> God's creature, and my fellow [who works in the field
> and is not a student] is God's creature. My work is in
> the town, and his work is in the country. I rise early for
> my work, and he rises early for his work. Just as he
> does not presume to do my work, so I do not pre-
> sume to do his work. Will you say, I do much [in the
> study of Torah] and he does little? We have learned:
> One may do much or one may do little; it is all one,
> provided that the person directs his heart to heaven.[20]

With similar modesty, Gandhi argued that "a lawyer's work
has the same value as the barber's". He himself spent many
hours at the loom in physical rather than intellectual toil, and

once remarked: "a life of labour, i.e. the life of the tiller of the soil and the handicraftsman, is the life worth living."[21]

But what of "useless" occupations, like that described by al-Jabbar? What of the man who pours water "to no purpose from one part of the sea to another"? The world's faiths are slow to judge the labourer in such scenarios, and rather criticise the employer for offering demeaning work. Indeed, the focus of al-Jabbar's condemnation was the man who hired the water-pourer, not the worker himself.

Pope John Paul similarly criticised employers who treated their workers as "merchandise" — to be bought and sold with the same dignity as livestock. However, he stressed, such unscrupulous practices could not empty work of all its value because, he said, all work was carried out by man, and man was inherently valuable.[22]

Towards the end of his encyclical, the late Pope — who was something of a workaholic himself — returned to the question of: why? Why was work good? He concluded by quoting the Second Vatican Council:

> Just as human activity proceeds from man, so it is ordered towards man. For when a man works he not only alters things and society, he develops himself as well. He learns much, he cultivates his resources, he goes outside of himself and beyond himself. Rightly understood, this kind of growth is of greater value than any external riches which can be garnered . . .[23]

In short, labour is its own reward. The lesson can be drawn from *The Parable of the Three Servants* in Matthew's Gospel.[24] But it is perhaps better articulated in the following tale, which is attributed to Sufism but which also turns up — in a similar form — in *Aesop's Fables*:

> Once a farmer lay on his deathbed despairing of the fate of his lazy sons. Near his final hour, an inspiration came to him. He called his sons around his bedside and bade them draw in close. "I am soon to leave this world sons," he whispered. "I want you to know that I have left a treasure of gold for you. I have hidden it in my field. Dig carefully and well and you shall find it. I ask only that you share it amongst yourselves evenly."
>
> The sons begged him to tell them exactly where he had buried it, but the father breathed his last breath and spoke no more.
>
> As soon as their father was buried, the sons took up their pitchforks and shovels and began to turn over the soil in their father's field. They dug and dug until they had turned over the whole field twice. They found no treasure. But they decided that since the field was so well dug up they might as well plant some grain as their father had done. The crop grew well for them. After the harvest they decided to dig again in hopes of finding the buried treasure. Again they found not a treasure, but a field prepared for sowing. This year's crop was better than the one before.
>
> This went on for a number of years until the sons had grown accustomed to the cycles of the season and the rewards of daily labour. By that time their farming earned them each enough money to live a happy life. It was then that they realised the treasure their father had left for them.[25]

Endnotes

1 John Paul II (1981), *Laborem exercens*, p. 4.

2 John Paul II, *op. cit.* p. 28–9.

3 John Paul II, *op. cit.* p. 30.

4 *The Doctrine of the Mean* 20.

5 Keown, D. (2005), *Buddhist Ethics*, Oxford University Press, p.6.

6 Tang, C. (1996), *A Treasury of China's Wisdom*, Beijing: Foreign Languages Press, pp. 79–80.

7 Tang, C., *op. cit.*, p. 152–3.

8 Hadith of al-Bukhari as cited in Al-Qaradawi Y. (1994), *The Lawful and the Prohibited in Islam*, Indiana: American Trust Publications, p. 127.

9 Hourani G.F. (1971), *Islamic Rationalism: The Ethics of 'Abd al-Jabbar*, Oxford: Clarendon Press, pp. 75–6.

10 Cole G.D.H. (translator) (1973), *Jean-Jacques Rousseau: The Social Contract and Discourses*, London & Melbourne: Everyman, p. 16.

11 Weber, M. (1904/1930), *The Protestant Ethic and the Spirit of Capitalism* (translated by T. Parson), New York: Charles Scribner's Sons, p. 157–8.

12 A.N. Wilson (ed.) (1987), *The Lion and the Honeycomb: The Religious Writings of Tolstoy*, translated by Robert Chandler. London: Collins, p. 57.

13 A.N. Wilson (ed.), *op. cit.*, pp. 57–8.

14 Stevenson, R.L. (1876), *Apology for Idlers*.

15 *The Lao Tzu* 37.

16 *The Lao Tzu* 4.

17 John Paul II, *op. cit.*, p. 27.

18 Alexander Simpkins, C. and Simpkins A. (2000), *Simple Confucianism*. Massachusetts: Tuttle Publishing, p. 50.

19 Cited in Dorff, E.N. (2001), "Doing The Right and The Good: Fundamental Convictions and Methods of Jewish Ethics" in J. Runzo and N.M. Martin (eds.), *Ethics in the World Religions*. Oxford: Oneworld, p. 98.

20 Cited in Dorff, E.N., *op. cit.*, p. 98.

21 Gandhi, M.K. (1927), *An Autobiography*, Ahmedabad, India: Navajivan Trust, p. 250.

22 John Paul II, *op. cit.* pp. 6–7.

23 John Paul II, *op. cit.*, p. 29.

24 Matthew 25: 14–30.

25 Davy Pearmain, E. (1998), *Doorways to the Soul*, Cleveland, Ohio: The Pilgrim Press, p. 29.

12

LOVE

A woman, carrying her child, went to the future Buddha's tank to wash. And having first bathed the child, she put on her upper garment and descended into the water to bathe herself.

Then a Yakshini [demon], seeing the child, had a craving to eat it. And taking the form of a woman, she drew near, and asked the mother:

"Friend, this *is* a *very* pretty child, is it one of yours?"

And when she was told it was, she asked if she might nurse it. And this being allowed, she nursed it a little, and then carried it off.

But when the mother saw this, she ran after her, and cried out: "Where are you taking my child to?" and caught hold of her.

The Yakshini boldly said, "Where did you get the child from? It is mine!" And so quarrelling, they passed the door of the future Buddha's Judgement Hall.

He heard the noise, sent for them, inquired into
the matter, and asked them whether they would
abide by his decision. And they agreed. Then he had a
line drawn on the ground; and told the Yakshini to
take hold of the child's arms, and the mother to take
hold of its legs; and said: "The child shall be hers who
drags him over the line."

But as soon as they pulled at him, the mother, seeing how he suffered, grieved as if her heart would
break. And letting him go, she stood there weeping.

Then the future Buddha asked the bystanders:
"Whose hearts are tender to babes? Those who have
borne children, or those who have not?"

And they answered: "O Sire! The hearts of mothers are tender."

Then he said: "Who, think you, is the mother? She
who has the child in her arms, or she who has let go?"

And they answered: "She who has let go is the
mother" . . .

[Having exposed the Yakshini for what it was, the
future Buddha returned the child to his mother.]
[She] said: "O my Lord! O Great Physician! May thy
life be long!" And she went away, with her babe
clasped to her bosom."[1]

The virtue of love must be separated from its depiction in
popular culture. Love is neither lust nor desire. It is neither
passion nor pleasure. How could it be when the hallmark of
every virtue is difficulty, if not pain? The story above, which
has a Hebrew version in which Solomon plays the part of the
future Buddha, illustrates love from a religious viewpoint, and
indeed the viewpoint of right-thinking secular philosophers.
To love, in essence, is to put oneself last and the object of

one's love first. It is to do as the mother in the story did: disregard one's own interests — or, in other words, sacrifice oneself — for the sake of one's beloved.

Like other virtues, love — real love — is somewhat unfashionable today. All around us we are told by "life coaches" and other such self-help gurus to put our personal needs and desires first in relationships. "Co-dependence is a very real problem," says Seana McGee, a contemporary sex therapist, who rails against the "insidious martyrdom" of most marriages, and declares "chemistry" to be the most important thing in relationships. "The whole idea of basically prioritising other people's needs over ourselves as a virtuous philosophy ultimately sacrifices saneness and leads to addiction, cancer and rage disorders," she argues.[2]

But the fact that love is self-sacrifice is confirmed by the few convincing descriptions of the virtue in world literature. Take the Hindu epic of Sita and Rama, whose heroically erotic union transcends anything today's peddlers of self-centred love can offer. In one account of their courting, the couple came across a lotus pool on "a night of warmth and beauty". It is said:

> They plunged together into the cool, moon-swept waters, and Rama cast at his bride many fair water blooms . . .
> Hide-and-seek they then played amidst the floating flowers. Rama sank down until his face only was seen, and Sita, who searched for him, knew not whether she saw the face of Rama or a blue lotus bloom on the surface of the pond. Bending down to smell what seemed to be a flower, she touched her lover's lips, and he kissed her sweetly. Then Sita hid herself, and

> her face was like to a lotus bloom among lotus
> blooms. Rama kissed her many times ere she moved
> or smiled. . . . At length they darted merrily from the
> pond in bright moonlight, their garments dripping
> sparkling water drops, and then they drank cups of
> honey; the heart of Sita was intoxicated, and she bab-
> bled words of love and sweetness . . .[3]

Such frolicking revealed a bond between Rama and Sita. What
confirmed a love was how the couple risked their lives for one
another as their story unfolded. Rama bravely rescued his
wife from the clutches of the demon Ravana, and Sita threw
herself into a fire to prove to her husband her chastity.

A more extreme — and perhaps too extreme — form of
self-sacrifice is depicted in the western world's most celebrated ode to love: *Romeo and Juliet.* In Shakespeare's play,
hero and heroine commit suicide one after the other — so
devoted are they to their union. In Arab cultures, the sacrificial theme is played out too — one story telling of the heart-
broken Alya riding to the grave of her great love Aziz. There,
she "hurled herself off the saddle" onto a broken sword
which had been driven into the grave, and thus she "died on
the spot".[4]

Popular as such tales are, however, they celebrate a form
of love of questionable virtue. In taking their own lives, Juliet
and Alya seek to be reunited with their beloved. But with
what motivation? Quite possibly a selfish one: the desire to
be free from the pain of loss. All one can say is that the two
"heroines" come all-too-close to endorsing the grotesque
practice of *sati* in India. Although banned since 1829, *sati* (or
suttee) is still practised in isolated areas, drawing upon a

distorted account of the Sita legend in which the heroine is burnt alive on her husband's funeral pyre.

If Juliet and Alya represent one extreme of devotion, the Good Samaritan represents another, namely a form of devotion that fails to scale the heights of love. That may seem harsh on the character whom we met in the chapter on compassion. But, if love means anything, it means more than "doing unto others what you would wish done unto you". It means more than behaving "like a neighbour", as Jesus described the Good Samaritan.[5] It means more than applying the Golden Rule.

Returning to the story at the outset, we find perhaps the simplest definition of love: putting oneself last and one's beloved first. In applying the Golden Rule, one puts oneself and the object of one's compassion on the same level; one affords oneself and him, or her, equal concern. But in loving, one cares only for one's beloved.

At a minimum, therefore, love is self-denial: denial of one's own interests, and one's selfish impulses. As the poet Cesare Pavese remarked, looking at love from the other side of the fence, "You will be loved the day when you will be able to show your weakness without the person using it to assert his strength." Or, as the Lebanese poet Kahlil Gibran put it:

> For even as love crowns you so shall he crucify you
> . . . Like sheaves of corn he gathers you unto himself.
> He threshes you to make you naked. He sifts you to
> free you from your husks. He grinds you to white-
> ness. He kneads you until you are pliant; And then he
> assigns you to his sacrificial fire, that you may become
> sacred bread for God's sacred feast.[6]

St Paul also emphasised love's sacrificial nature but somewhat less lustily. He memorably wrote:

> Love is always patient and kind: it is never jealous;
> love is never boastful or conceited; it is never rude or
> selfish; it does not take offence, and is not resentful.
> Love takes no pleasure in other people's sins but de-
> lights in the truth; it is always ready to excuse, to
> trust, to hope, and to endure whatever comes.[7]

In his letter to the Corinthians, St Paul also suggested that love was the supreme virtue, if not the only virtue that mattered. As the disciple said:

> If I have all the eloquence of men or of angels, but
> speak without love, I am simply a gong booming or a
> cymbal clashing. If I have the gift of prophecy, under-
> standing all the mysteries there are, and knowing eve-
> rything, and if I have faith in all its fullness, to move
> mountains, but without love, then I am nothing at all. If
> I give away all that I possess, piece by piece, and if I
> even let them take my body to burn it, but am without
> love, it will do me no good whatever.[8]

Echoing such thoughts, St Augustine asked: "Does love bring about the keeping of the commandments, or does the keeping of the commandments bring about love?" And he answered: "But who can doubt that love comes first? For the one who does not love has no reason for keeping the commandments."[9]

So love is a crucial — and a demanding — virtue, particularly in Christianity. But love of what? Jesus described love of the world as a sin. Instead of loving it, he said:

> "Love the Lord your God with all your heart, with all your soul, and with all your mind." This is the greatest and most important commandment. The second most important commandment is like it: "Love your neighbour as you love yourself." The whole Law of Moses and the teachings of the prophets depend on these two commandments.[10]

Critically, love of God comes first in Jesus' book. Secular humanists wish it weren't the case, believing the second form of love to be sustainable without the first. But theirs is mere wishful thinking from the Christian viewpoint. As Tolstoy wrote: "It would indeed be extremely advantageous if people were able to love humanity", as advocated by "the champions of Positivist, Socialist and Communist brotherhood". However, "What they propose is love for humanity alone, without love for God. And such a love cannot exist. There is no motivation for it," said Tolstoy. "Christian love can spring only from a Christian understanding of life, an understanding where the meaning of life lies in the love and service of God."[11]

Other faiths lend themselves to a similar conclusion. In Judaism and Sufism, everything stems from the love of God. Indeed, more so than Christianity, both faiths celebrate divine love poetry — poetry sometimes bordering on the erotic — in the course of their worship.

The Sufi mystic Rabi'a al-'Adawiya (d. 801) scandalised orthodox Muslims in her day by refusing to marry, seeking "union" instead with God. "The contract of marriage is for those who have a phenomenal existence," she said. "But in my case there is no such existence, for I have ceased to exist and have passed out of self. I exist in God and am altogether His. I live in the shadow of His command. The marriage contract must be asked from Him, not from me."[12]

The like-minded Abu Yazid al-Bistami (d. 874) also approached God as a lover. The Sufi mystic "believed that he should strive to please Allah as he would a woman in a human love affair, sacrificing his own needs and desires so as to become one with the Beloved."[13]

Muid al-Din ibn al-Arabi (1165–1240) pushed the boat out further, likening his feelings for God to the sense of emotion which overwhelmed him on the *hajj* in Mecca when he had a vision of a young girl named Nizam. Inspired by the heavenly sight, he declared: "If you love a being for his beauty, you love none other than God, for he is *the* Beautiful Being. . . . Thus in all its aspects, the object of love is God alone." [14]

In Christian Italy, the poet Dante Alighieri (1265–1321) saw God in a childhood sweetheart, named Beatrice. This Florentine girl became the ultimate "God-bearing image" who led Dante out of Hell in *The Divine Comedy*. He wrote:

> I say that when she appeared from any direction, then, in the hope of her wondrous salutation, there was no enemy left to me; rather there smote into me a flame of charity, which made me forgive every person who had ever injured me; and if at that moment anybody had put a question to me about anything whatsoever, my answer would have been simply "Love", with a countenance clothed in humility.[15]

It is perhaps no coincidence that Beatrice eluded Dante's grasp (she married a banker and died young) for, as Plato observed, we love what we lack.[16] Al-Arabi, whose Nizam proved similarly elusive, reached the same conclusion. Love, he believed, was "essentially a yearning for something that remains absent".[17]

While Dante's writings were considered blasphemous in his day, he was, in fact, continuing a tradition of humanising man's love of God. The *Song of Solomon*, or *Song of Songs*, in the Old Testament, or Hebrew Bible, gives a vivid picture of erotic love between a man and a woman, albeit theologians continue to debate just who exactly the pair are meant to represent: God and his people? Or, perhaps, the institution of marriage? However, the case for viewing the "song" as an allegory for the worship of God is strengthened by other passages in the Bible endorsing affection for the divine. Reading Psalms, we proclaim: "As a hart [deer] longs for flowing streams, so longs my soul for thee, O God."[18]

Some mystical texts of Judaism go further by giving God a physical appearance, thereby making him all the more loveable. "My beloved is fresh and ruddy," runs one such text;

> His head is golden, purest gold, his locks are palm fronds and black as the raven. His eyes are doves at a pool of water, bathed in milk, at rest on a pool; his cheeks are beds of spices, banks sweetly scented. His lips are lilies, distilling pure myrrh. His hands are golden, rounded, set with jewels of Tarshish. His belly a block of ivory covered with sapphires. His legs are alabaster columns.[19]

No less controversially, the Zohar — the central text of Kabbalah, the most influential strand of Jewish mysticism — likens the Torah, the first five books of the Hebrew Bible (or the Christian Old Testament), to something of a flirt.

> When the Torah uncovers a matter, it is revealed
> for a moment but is immediately concealed again.
> Such revelation is granted only to those who know
> her and are capable of recognising her value.
>
> To what may this be compared? It is like a woman,
> beautiful, gracious, and much loved, who is kept con-
> fined in her palace . . . She opens a secret opening in
> the palace where she dwells and reveals her face to
> her lover, only to withdraw immediately and become
> concealed again. No-one in her lover's vicinity sees or
> understands. Only her lover knows, and he yearns for
> her with his whole being, heart and soul, for he
> knows that it was out of love for him that she re-
> vealed herself to him for one moment in order to
> awaken his love.[20]

As for Buddhism, while its followers might object to Cardinal
Ratzinger's description of the faith as "auto-erotic", it does
depart from the Judeo-Christian tradition in advocating self-
love above all other manifestations of the virtue. That is not
to say that Buddhism condones selfishness. Quite the reverse:
self-love is considered by Buddhists to be a prerequisite for
loving others. As the future Buddha says in one *Jakata* tale:

> Since, then, so dear is each man to himself,
> Let him that loveth self none other harm.[21]

Specifically, Buddhists are encouraged to generate feelings of
"loving kindness", one of the "four measureless states". Like
Jesus, the Buddha discouraged people from limiting the scope
of their love, calling ultimately for a "boundless friendly mind
for all creatures".[22] In pursuance of this end, Buddhists engage
in a contemplative exercise. This starts with thinking about

oneself and then passing through one's close friends and family to those one dislikes until one finally embraces the whole universe and all the beings within it. A similar exercise is performed in Christianity where one prays for one's immediate family and friends, as well as oneself, before extending the prayer to strangers, and ultimately the whole world.

Confucianism shares with Buddhism an emphasis on self-love. Believing that people who despised themselves would inevitably be despised by others, Mencius advocated what he called "self-cultivation". In a lesson repeated by self-help gurus down the ages, he said one should tend to oneself lovingly as one would to a plant:

> Anyone who really wishes to grow a small tree like the t'ung or szu tree learns how to tend to it. But in the matter of one's own person, there are those who do not learn how to tend it, not so much because they have a greater love for a tree than for themselves, but because of a heedlessness that is very deep-seated.[23]

But Confucianism, like Buddhism, frowns upon self-love if it excludes loving others. In fact, Confucius regarded love of virtue — rather than love of self — as the highest form of love. "Better than one who knows what is right is one who is fond of what is right," he said. "And better than one who is fond of what is right is one who delights in what is right."[24]

Significantly, Confucianism — like Christianity — features an anti-rationalist streak. According to Confucian thought, one can't love humanity until one loves the Mandate of Heaven. But in what is it grounded? A dozen years after Tolstoy (1828–1910) had argued that the "champions of Positivist, Socialist and Communist brotherhood" were selling a lie,

Wang Kuo-wei (1877–1927) observed that one couldn't correct that lie by making positivism, socialism or communism loveable. The one-time scholar of western philosophy, who gave up his interest in Schopenhauer and Kant in order to return to his Confucian roots, wrote: "I have been tired of philosophy for a considerable time. Among philosophical theories, it is a general rule that those that can be loved cannot be believed, and those that can be believed cannot be loved. I know truth, and yet I love absurd yet great metaphysics, sublime ethics, and pure aesthetics. These are what I love most. Yet in searching for what is believable, I am inclined to believe in the positivistic theory of truth, the hedonistic theory of ethics, and the empiricist theory of aesthetics. I know these are believable, but I cannot love them, and I feel the other theories are loveable, but I cannot believe in them."[25]

Thus the world's faiths collectively celebrate not just love but *love of God*, or its equivalent — be it the self as part of a greater whole, or a divine equivalent to God, like the Mandate of Heaven. Moreover, the world's religions suggest that love of God (or its equivalent) is the primary form of love, and from it all other manifestations of the virtue flow.

Islam is sometimes singled out as an exception in this regard but with what validity? It is argued (mostly by non-Muslims) that love is a principally Christian virtue, somewhat alien to Islamic teaching. For a start, the argument goes, God is rarely portrayed as a loving God in the Qur'an. Of the 99 names attributed to Allah in orthodox Islam the majority describe a deity of somewhat frightening authority. The Tremendous, The Powerful, The All-Compelling Subduer, The Omniscient, The Judge, The Majestic, The Strong, and The

Avenger are among the awe-inspiring titles attached to Islam's God. The Loving One and The Giver of Life are among Allah's other titles but some (again, mainly non-Muslims) would say, almost as an afterthought. What is fair comment is that Muslims tend to describe Islam as a religion of peace rather than a religion of love, reflecting perhaps its strong focus on the virtue of justice. Moreover, Islamic leaders generally speak of fearing God rather than loving Him as the most appropriate form of worship. Of the Islamic mindset, Ruthven comments: "Love, it would seem, belongs to the human sphere. The all-embracing cosmic deity conveyed in the Qur'an cannot be apprehended closely enough to elicit the warmth of love in the average human."[26]

Not all Muslims agree, however, and Sufis disagree more than most. The aforementioned woman mystic Rabi'a of Basra reportedly walked around the streets of her home town with a flaming torch in one hand and a jar of water in the other. When asked to explain herself, she replied, "I want to quench the fires of hell with the water and burn down paradise with the torch, so that people can come to love God selflessly, neither out of fear of the one nor out of greed for the other."[27]

Not surprisingly Sufi Muslims have been attracted to the teachings of the prophet Jesus. One Islamic story — of likely Sufi origin — tells of Jesus coming across a large group of worshippers who had "shrivelled up from worshipping, like worn-out water skins":

> "Who are you?" he asked. "We are worshippers,"
> they answered. "Why do you worship?" he asked.
> They replied, "God put the fear of hell in us, and we

were afraid." So he said, "It is incumbent upon God to save you from what you fear." Then Jesus passed on and came upon others who were even more worshipful. He asked, "Why do you worship?" and they replied, "God gave us a longing for paradise and what He has prepared there for His friends. That is what we hope for." So Jesus said, "It is incumbent upon God to give you what you hope for." Then he passed them by and came upon others who were worshipping and said, "Who are you?" They said, "We are lovers of God. We worship Him not out of fear of hell or longing for paradise, but out of love for Him and to His greater glory." So Jesus said, "You are truly the friends of God, and it is with you that I was commanded to live." And he resided among them.[28]

The contrast between Christianity (along with Sufism) and orthodox Islam is most acute in the telling of the creation myth surrounding the fall of Adam. In the Christian account, Adam is stricken with feelings of guilt and remorse after taking the forbidden fruit in the Garden of Eden. Once banished from paradise, he must live with the shame until death. In the Islamic account, however:

> Adam is a model of the true Muslim. He failed, yes, but he also repented and turned back to God; not out of guilt but out of fear (*taqwaa*). He feared God, as all true Muslims should. And God forgave Adam.[29]

Are the two approaches to God necessarily in conflict, however? By fearing God, as Muslims do, one sacrifices oneself to God's authority. But by loving God (affectionately), as Christians do, one is also surrendering to His will. Christians and Muslims might disagree over the terminology but at the heart of each faith is the same commitment: to put oneself last, and one's beloved first. The very word Islam is an exhortation in this regard, literally translating as "surrender to God". As for Christianity, Jesus told his disciples: "If anyone wants to come with me, he must forget self, carry his cross, and follow me."[30] No doubt St Paul has these words in mind when he spoke of kenosis, or self-emptying, as the key teaching of the faith.

Is Christian love, then, the same virtue as Islamic "surrender"? In its relationship with God, perhaps. But recall what Jesus said: that, having loved God, you should love your neighbour as yourself. This second-order love does not feature in Islam. There is no plea for "surrender" to one's neighbour; one should apply justice, compassion and other virtues in human affairs, but no more.

What, however, did Jesus mean when he said, "Love your neighbour as you love yourself"? Nowhere in the Bible did he give us an explicit explanation. As mentioned before, he praised the Good Samaritan for having "acted like a neighbour". But that falls short of the ideal.

Indeed, the more one thinks about it, the more impossible "loving one's neighbour as oneself" seems. As for loving one's enemies — a subject to be addressed in the next chapter — surely we are in the realm of fantasy? And yet there it is, at the heart of Judaeo-Christian teaching: a plea for universal love; not just empathy or compassion, charity or justice, but love.

Is there a story in which someone loves his neighbour as himself? Christians might reply, "Yes, the story of Jesus." But how do we learn from that today? Reading about universal love is not the same as practising it. At some stage we must put the books down and try to live the ideal. There is, in

other words, only one way of finding out whether Jesus —
and like-minded prophets — were selling us a lie. It is told:

> A man sent his son to the *yeshiva*, the Talmudic acad-
> emy, to study Talmud for five years. When he re-
> turned the father met him, took him aside into his
> study and asked him what he had learnt. The son re-
> plied: "I learnt that the greatest teaching is 'you shall
> love your neighbour as yourself'." "But you knew that
> before you went away!" said the father. "You didn't
> need five years of study to find that out!" "The differ-
> ence," said the son, "is that now I know what it
> means: 'I must love *my* neighbour as myself'!"[31]

Endnotes

[1] Rhys-Davids, C.A.F. (1998), *Buddhist Birth-Stories*, New Delhi: Srishti Publishers and Distributors, pp. xii–xv.

[2] *The Irish Times*, 10 June 2002.

[3] Mackenzie D.A. (1913), *Indian Myth and Legend*, London: Gresham Publishing, pp. 384–5.

[4] El-Shamy H.M. (1999), *Tales Arab Women Tell and the Behavioral Patterns They Portray*, Bloomington & Indianapolis: Indiana University Press, pp. 350-5.

[5] Luke 10: 25–37.

[6] Gibran, K. (1926) The Prophet, Arrow Books: London, p.11.

[7] Corinthians 13:1–13.

[8] *ibid*.

[9] John Paul II (1993), *Veritatis Spendor*, London: Catholic Trust Society, p. 37.

[10] Matthew 22:34–40.

[11] A.N. Wilson (ed.) (1987), *The Lion and the Honeycomb: The Religious Writings of Tolstoy*, translated by Robert Chandler. London: Collins, pp. 85–6.

[12] Ruthven, M. (2000), *Islam in the World*, New York: Oxford University Press, p. 225.

[13] Armstrong, K. (1999), *A History of God*, London: Vintage, p. 261.

[14] Armstrong, K., *op. cit.*, pp. 270–1.

[15] Sayers, D.L. (translator) (1949), Dante, *The Divine Comedy (Hell)*, Middlesex: Penguin, p. 28.

[16] Plato, *Symposium*, 220e.

[17] Armstrong, K., *op. cit.*, p. 271.

[18] Psalms 42:1.

[19] From the Shiur Qomah, "The Measurement of the Height", as cited in Armstrong, K., *op. cit.*, pp. 248–9.

[20] From the Zohar as cited in Richards, C. (1997), *Illustrated Encyclopaedia of World Religions*, Dorset: Element Books, p. 62.

[21] Woodward, F.L. (1925), *Buddhist Stories*. Madras, India: Theosophical Publishing House, pp. 27–31.

[22] Garrett Jones, J. (1979), *Tales and Teachings of the Buddha*, London: George Allen & Unwin, p. 115.

[23] Alexander Simpkins, C. and Simpkins, A. (2000), *Simple Confucianism*, Massachusetts: Tuttle Publishing, p. 20.

[24] Alexander Simpkins, C. and Simpkins, A. *op. cit.*, p. 75.

[25] Fung Yu-Lan (1948), *A Short History of Chinese Philosophy*, New York: The Free Press, p. 327.

[26] Ruthven, M., *op. cit.*, p. 221.

[27] Khalidi, T. (2001), *The Muslim Jesus*, Cambridge, Massachusetts: Harvard University Press, p. 141.

[28] Khalidi, T., *op. cit.*, p. 140.

[29] Fashing, D.J. and Dechant D. (2001), *Comparative Religious Ethics*, Massachusetts: Blackwell, p. 237.

[30] Matthew 16:24.

[31] Magonet, J. (1995), "Judaism and a Global Ethic" in Küng, H. (ed.) (1995), *Yes to a Global Ethic*, London: SCM Press, p. 96.

13

JUSTICE

JUSTICE

A group of kings living next to Muslim lands once decided to test Islamic justice. So they sent a minister to Istanbul, and told him to ride a fine black stallion outside of the palace of the sultan. But the minister was told that under no circumstances should he sell the horse to the sultan, and if the animal was seized by force to appeal to the *shari'a* court.

Sure enough, the stallion caught the attention of the sultan who offered vast sums of money for the horse. But the minister would not yield, and the horse was seized instead. As planned, the minister then went to the *shari'a* court and complained to the *qadi*. The *qadi* convened a sitting of the court in the presence of the sultan, and told the minister to state his claim.

"Tell me first," said the minister, who was standing by the door, "does your Qur'anic law rule that the sultan may sit near your lordship in the place of honour, while I must crouch here where every man that enters kicks off his shoes?" The *qadi* ordered the sultan to stand next to the minister and went on, "What is the accusation?" The minister replied, "The sultan has taken my stallion. I want neither money nor horses in its stead. I only want my horse back."

"Does he speak the truth?" the *qadi* asked of the sultan. "Yes, that is what happened," said the sultan.

The *qadi* gave his judgement: he ruled that the sultan must return the stallion to its owner. The sultan nodded his turban with approval. "Justly spoken," he said. "Had you ruled otherwise, O *qadi* of the court, I would have cut off your head with this sword!" "And had you disregarded the decision of the *shari'a* court, O sultan," said the *qadi*, "had you broken the law of the Qur'an and made light of my judgement, I should have let this viper destroy you and turn you to ashes." And he lifted the corner of the mat on which he sat and revealed the snake in a bag beneath it.[1]

Justice is a multifaceted concept that acts as shorthand for any number of virtues. On one level, to be "just" is to be "right". We speak of people being "honest and just", "merciful and just" or "compassionate and just" to emphasise their honesty, mercy or compassion. But what does it mean to be just in its own right?

To answer this question from a religious perspective we need to go back to the Golden Rule, arguably the key moral law in each faith. Recall that the world's main religions declare, albeit all in their own idiosyncratic way, "Do unto others as you would wish done unto you." Obeying this rule in the context of helping a person in need can be described as compassion. But obeying it in other situations of a social or political nature best translates as "fairness" — an ethical concept which, along with equality, closely relates to justice in both religious and secular philosophies. Aristotle, for example, defined justice as "lawful and fair", while John Rawls, arguably the most influential political philosopher of the last half-century, described it as a form of "fair play" based on principles of liberty and equality.

The central place of justice in western philosophy has, of course, much to do with the fact that the virtue has been a key concern of western religion. Throughout the annals of Judaism, Christianity and Islam, we find episodes of injustice condemned by God and His representatives on earth. In freeing the Hebrews from slavery and leading them on an exodus to Mount Sinai, Moses began what was perhaps the first organised political movement in history — a movement directed against the unjust rule of the then King of Egypt. Jesus, sometimes dubbed "the world's first socialist", preached against all types of injustices, from the hypocrisy of the scribes and Pharisees, to the hoarding of riches in an unequal world. As for Muhammad, he articulated what some would argue was a more rigorous case for equality and fairness. In his farewell sermon, the Prophet reportedly declared:

> An Arab has no superiority over a non-Arab nor a non-Arab has any superiority over an Arab; also a white has no superiority over a black nor a black has any superiority over a white — except by piety and good action. Learn that every Muslim is a brother to every Muslim and that the Muslims constitute one brotherhood. Nothing shall be legitimate to a Muslim which belongs to a fellow Muslim unless it was given freely and willingly.[2]

While justice has a place in each tradition, however, it would be wrong to say that all western faiths, let alone all world religions, have the same conception of the virtue. Each tradition has its own specific concerns, and perhaps more significantly, its own perception of human history. Just what you believe is unjust depends greatly on what you think went before, and what you think is achievable in the future. For each faith, the devil is in the detail, and, thus, perhaps the best way of understanding justice in the world's main religions is to scrutinise how they approach one specific type of apparent wrongdoing: physical violence.

Consider Christianity and Islam first: two monotheisms drawn from the same Abrahamic religious family but nonetheless widely assumed to be in conflict. The former, preaching the idealistic, and some might say, unrealistic, ethic of "love your enemy", is said to stand in contrast with the latter, a faith born with a heightened sense of righteous indignation and a fervour for social change. As the religious scholar Malise Ruthven puts it, "whereas Christianity is primarily the religion of love, Islam is above all the religion of justice."[3]

One would certainly be drawn to this conclusion if one compared how Jesus and Muhammad tackled injustice in their own lives. Where Jesus accepted his persecution in a spirit of self-sacrifice, Muhammad fought back against those who tried to assassinate him, fleeing from Mecca to Medina where he regrouped and built an army that delivered Islam's bloody birth.

Ambush, assassination and massacre were among the tactics used by Muhammad to achieve his goal. At Badr, he had the wells of his enemies filled in, forcing them to fight, tired

and thirsty, on ground of his choosing. The head of the
Quraishi leader Abu Jahl was severed from his body after the
battle and brought to Muhammad who gave thanks to Allah.

It is perhaps because of changing sensitivities within Islam
that the Prophet tends to be distanced from such bloodshed
in the retelling of Islamic legends. In a description of one battle, for example, Ali kills an enemy leader by slicing him in
two equal halves, "and his horse as well." Mikdad, a compan-
ion of Ali's, slices off heads "like plums from a tree late in the
season". Muhammad, in contrast, fights by throwing pebbles,
or grains of sand, each one miraculously deadly in its effect.[4]

But neither the Prophet's role in the war, nor his sanc-
tioning of the methods used therein, can be ignored. "Without the sword there would be no respect for Muhammad's
law," runs one Islamic proverb.[5]

The contrast with Jesus — perhaps the first pacifist in the
western world — is stark. In Matthew's Gospel, Christ spells
out his philosophy:

> You have heard that it was said, "An eye for an
> eye and a tooth for a tooth." But I say to you: Do not
> resist one who is evil. But if any one strikes you on
> the right cheek, turn to him the other also; and if any
> one would sue you and take your coat, let him have
> your cloak as well . . .
> You have heard that it was said, "You shall love
> your neighbour and hate your enemy." But I say to
> you: Love your enemies and pray for those who per-
> secute you. . . . For if you love those who love you,
> what reward have you? Do not even the tax collec-
> tors do the same? And if you salute only your breth-
> ren, what more are you doing than others? Do not

even the Gentiles do the same? You, therefore, must
be perfect, as your heavenly Father is perfect.[6]

Jesus taught perfection, and indeed lived it. But, then, Jesus —
so Christianity would tell us — was the Son of God, and Muhammad never claimed to be anything other than a human
being. Tellingly, the prophet Jesus is portrayed in Islamic literature as a more human — and fallible — character, seeking
retribution against his enemies and avoiding self-sacrifice on
the cross. "Muslims do not believe that Jesus was crucified
because they regard that as shameful," according to one
scholar of Islamic legend. "Crucified means cursed (*mal-un*),
and this was done only to evil sprits who would never receive God's grace."[7] In the Muslim account of Jesus' persecution, an attempt was made to crucify the prophet but he was
liberated from his bonds by the angel Jibril (Gabriel). The ropes
in which he had been tied "just disintegrated". Afterwards, a
wicked king, called Tastum (who equates to Judas in the Biblical story) went to the jail to see the imprisoned prophet, only
to find his cell empty.

> At that moment the Almighty changed his appearance
> so that the king looked exactly like Jesus, whereupon
> the people assaulted him and beat him to death,
> laughing at his protests that he was their king. When
> he had died, however, God changed his features back,
> so that the rabble suddenly realised they had killed
> their own king. They started accusing each other and
> a fight broke out in which many died.[8]

The Christian commandment to "turn the other cheek" is
reworked in another Muslim story, telling of the prophet's

journey with a disciple to the Pass of Afiq, leading to the River Jordan:

> A man crossed their path and prevented them from proceeding, saying, "I will not let you pass until I have struck each of you a blow." They tried to dissuade him but he refused. Jesus said, "Here is my cheek. Slap it." The man slapped it and let him pass. He then said to the disciple, "I will not let you pass until I have slapped you too." The disciple refused. When Jesus saw this, he offered him his other cheek. He slapped it and allowed both to go. Jesus then said, "O God, if this is pleasing to You, your pleasure has reached me. If it does not please You, You are more worthy of righteous anger."[9]

The moral of the story is very much Islamic rather than Christian. While Jesus volunteers to take a blow for another, he does so with the qualification that God — if He so wills — will take revenge for the affront. In short, Jesus utters — all too humanly — a curse on his foe after being struck twice without justification.

One might ask whether Islam is a more practical — if not a more honest — religion than Christianity by encouraging its followers to emulate the example of a human being rather than a saint. It could be argued that, by calling on people to love their enemy, Christianity demands an unrealistic and, therefore, phoney ethic. After all, were it desirable for Christians to love their enemies, when would they ever do it?

Tolstoy asked the same question in his religious diaries, recalling vividly a conversation with a Jewish rabbi who found

equivalent references in the Talmud to all key teaching in the
Bible with the exception of Matthew 5:39. Tolstoy recalled:

> . . . when we came to the verse about non-resistance
> to evil, instead of saying "That is in the Talmud too",
> he simply asked mockingly, "Is that what Christians
> do? Do they turn the other cheek?" There was noth-
> ing I could answer; I knew that Christians at that time
> were not only not turning the other cheek, but hitting
> cheeks that Jews had turned. . . . By this question he
> implied that the presence of this law in the Christian
> code, a law that is not only never followed but even
> admitted by Christians themselves to be impractica-
> ble, was an admission of the irrationality and irrele-
> vance of the whole code.[10]

While Tolstoy initially had no reply for the rabbi, he eventually concluded that the strength of the Christian ethic was its
very impracticality. He wrote:

> Christ's teaching differs from earlier teachings in that
> it guides people not through external rules, but
> through an inner consciousness of the possibility of
> reaching divine perfection. . . . Only the aspiration
> towards this perfection is enough to take the direc-
> tion of man's life away from the animal condition and
> — as far as is possible in this life — towards the di-
> vine condition. . . . Only the ideal of absolute perfec-
> tion can influence people and motivate them to ac-
> tion. Moderate perfection has no power to act on
> men's souls.[11]

Whether the "moderate" perfection of Muhammad or the
divine perfection of Jesus is more persuasive in turning people

towards a moral life is debated by Christians and Muslims. Here, however, is not the place to settle the dispute. Rather, we need to take from this discussion an appreciation of the differences and similarities between the Islamic and Christian conceptions of justice. And, yes, there are *similarities* as well as differences. While Jesus and Muhammad may have reacted in polar-opposite ways to injustice in their own lives, the same cannot be said for the faiths, and followers, which they inspired. Both Christianity and Islam acknowledge the virtue of justice. Both also forbid the indiscriminate use of force.

Let's look at Islam first. Justice within the faith somewhat resembles the virtue promoted by Aristotle, Rawls, and many another philosopher, in that it calls for equality and fairness. According to Islamic teaching, Muslims have an unequivocal social responsibility to one another — a responsibility expressed, for instance, in compulsory charity, or *zakat*. Islamic justice, in the first instance, is not about punishing wrongdoers but about creating the conditions where punishment, or the imposition of force, is unnecessary. Consider how the first Muslims approached the crime of infanticide — a crime inextricably linked to poverty. Instead of sermonising about how sinful it was to kill one's children, Islam set about creating the social and economic conditions that would make such murder an unnecessary abomination. "Kill not your children in fear of impoverishment," the Qur'an declares. "We will provide for them and for you."[12]

As well as creating an interdependent community, or *umma*, Islam under Muhammad broke from traditional Arab forms of law-enforcement and conflict resolution. In the pre-Islamic "Age of Ignorance", justice meant killing your enemy before he killed you. The classic Arab hero at the time was Antar, a slave-turned-prince who fought by brutal and bloody means to increase his reputation and expand his fortune. Under Bedouin rules of combat, the man who failed to retaliate was not merciful nor enlightened but cowardly, and that was something of which Antar could never have been accused. Winning was all that mattered to the warrior prince who once remarked:

> He who lives for a day after the death of his foe has attained the goal he strove to attain.[13]

These words were uttered moments after Antar himself had killed an enemy whose final act was to shoot a poisoned arrow through Antar's scrotum, which would claim the hero's life some five months and five days later. There would be no final, death-bed conversion to "reason" for Antar. His last wish was for his family to avenge his death against a rival tribe. "Leave not a man of them alive," he uttered before expiring.[14]

Muhammad, in contrast, recommended mediation rather than violence when conflict occurred. He himself acted as a go-between when rival Bedouin tribes threatened to bring war to the holy city of Mecca, and in doing so he set an example for his followers. "It is more preferable to err with consultation than to do right with despotism," observed ʿAbd al-Malik, one of the early caliphs of Islam.[15] Critically, however, Muhammad gave his consent to violence when the chances of mediation had been exhausted. According to traditional Islamic teaching, the Prophet did not seek the original "holy war" against unbelievers. Rather, it was brought about by the intransigence of his rivals, and their unwillingness to let Muslims live in peace.

The story at the opening of this chapter fairly summarises Islamic justice (in its ideal form), for not only does it emphasise both fairness and equality, and specifically equality before the law, but it advocates mediation as a means of conflict resolution rather than force. Crucially, however, force is presented as a necessary last resort — and this is only right, according to Islamic teaching. "To those against whom war is made, permission is given [to fight], because they are wronged," says the Qur'an.[16] However, it makes clear force should only be used in limited circumstances.

In the words of one religious scholar, Islam permits violence only under these four conditions: first, if there is a grave and sudden threat to the faith; second, if Muslims are subjected to oppression; third, if Muslims are forced out of their land; or fourth, "when political entities commit deliberate breaches of treaties and pacts".[17] Under a more nuanced "just war" theory cited by other Islamic scholars, Muslim participation in *jihad* is allowed only if the war is in a just cause and declared by a legitimate authority. According to this theory, there must also be a reasonable hope of success, and the goal must be the reestablishment of peace. In addition, "prudential reasoning" should be a part of any military strategy, a condition associated with the proportional use of force.[18]

An underlying guide for all Muslims is the Qur'anic command not to take human life "which Allah hath made sacred" except in the pursuit of justice.[19] "Those against whom war is made . . . are wronged," runs one Qur'anic verse.[20] "Fight in the cause of Allah those who fight you, but do not transgress limits; for Allah loveth not transgressors."[21]

"Transgression" in this verse is sometimes translated as "aggression", suggesting Islamic *jihad*, or war, should only be defensive in nature. Yet another Qur'anic verse states: "He who killed any person, unless it be a person guilty of man-slaughter, or of spreading chaos in the land, should be looked upon as though he had slain all mankind, and he who saved one life should be regarded as though he had saved the lives of all mankind."[22] The verse bears a striking resemblance to a famous passage of the Jewish Mishnah, where the implications of God's creating humanity through Adam are spelt out. "First, killing one person is also killing all of his or her poten-tial descendants — indeed, 'an entire world'. Conversely, someone who saves an individual 'saves an entire world'."[23]

It should be noted that Judaism has also developed a tra-dition of "just war" theory. Indeed, its tradition arguably be-gan first, stemming originally from the Torah which urged Jews to give their foes a chance to surrender before besieging them.[24] Today, Jewish scholars today tend to speak of two types of war: obligatory and discretionary. The former are wars fought because God commanded Israel to wage them. The latter are wars either aimed at stopping aggressors, or are otherwise self-defensive in nature. According to tradi-tional teaching, discretionary wars are permissible after con-sultation but only if consent has been given by the relevant legal or administrative authority. As in Islam (and indeed Christianity), there are differences of opinion over the crite-ria for a "just war", not to mention how those criteria apply in practice. Among the more controversial Jewish concepts is *rodef* law, which allows someone to kill a Jew who imperils the life or property of another Jew. Conservative Jews have found justification for this law in the Talmud, and some even used it to incite anger against the former Israeli prime minister Yitzhak Rabin after his signing of the 1993 Oslo peace accord. Rabin, who was assassinated by an ultra-orthadox religious zealot in November 1995, had been labelled a traitor and a *rodef* for making concessions to the Palestinians.

Other Jewish scholars highlight texts that promote pacifism, or the minimisation of violence in conflict scenarios. One such scholar writes: "If one can stop a murderer from committing his crime without the use of deadly force, deadly force is prohibited; if one can separate combatants without using physical force, non-violent means are certainly preferred."[25]

Scholars of Islam similarly debate the criteria for a "just war". But there are grounds for arguing that the philosophy of the Qur'an is closer to one of pacifism than violence. One verse of the book advises that "if the enemy incline towards peace, do thou [also] incline towards peace, and trust in Allah".[26] Another verse — which has echoes of Matthew 5:39 — declares: "Repel evil with that which is best".[27] While the Qur'an might not command Muslims to love their enemies, they are urged to consider it a possibility. "It may be that Allah will grant love [and friendship] between you and those whom ye [now] hold as enemies. For Allah has power [over all things]; And Allah is Oft-Forgiving, Most Merciful."[28]

The final passage, emphasising the omnipotence of God, is critical to Muslim thought, and fully in keeping with a cautionary approach to justice. Whatever account of justice humankind agrees upon will always be imperfect compared to divine justice.

Christianity preaches a similar message, warning against rushing to blame. "Do not judge others, so that God will not judge you," said Jesus, for whom justice was inseparable from virtues like mercy and tolerance.[29] In Matthew's Gospel, he went further, however, than advocating caution in the administration of justice. Instead, he recommended subversion. "If anyone slaps you on the right cheek, let him slap your left cheek too."

But such appeals for pacifism must be seen in the context of Jesus' other teachings, particularly those on peace-making, and loving one's neighbour as oneself. In the words of Dietrich Bonhoeffer (1905–1945), the German theologian who tried to assassinate Hitler, "If we took the precept of non-resistance as an ethical blueprint for general application, we should indeed be indulging in idealistic dreams. . . . To make non-resistance a principle for secular life is to deny God by undermining his gracious ordinance for the preservation of the world."[30]

The earliest Christian churches came to a similar conclusion, finding within the Bible evidence of a just-war theory, most famously elaborated by Saint Augustine. It was his belief that all wars were sinful and could only be waged in "a mournful spirit". However, he accepted the command to love one's neighbour included a duty to defend the vulnerable against attack.

Augustine's theory was developed and refined in later years and theologians now speak of seven conditions justifying a decision to go to war: there must be a just cause; war must be waged by a legitimate authority; it must be formally declared; those waging it must have a right intention; it must be the last resort; there must be reasonable hope of success; and there must be a due proportion between the benefits sought and the damage done.

What theoretical difference, then, is there between Islamic and Christian justice? Despite the contrasting examples of Jesus and Muhammad, both faiths warn against judgementalism, teaching that only God ultimately has the right to judge. Both advocate non-violent means of conflict resolution, call it peacemaking or mediation. And both allow force to be used in the pursuit of justice but only in limited circumstances, or when certain criteria are met. One might have thought religious leaders would build on these grounds to try to develop a shared understanding of justice. But instead they tend to concentrate on what divides them, an approach that can lead to name-calling or the deliberate misrepresentation of the doctrinal teachings of rival faiths. Some Christian leaders portray Islam as a violent faith that condones latter-day terrorism, while their Islamic counterparts argue that Christian "pacifism" implies indifference to social evils like inequality. The only thing upon which such peddlers of misrepresentation agree is how to disparage the concept of justice in Judaism, portraying Deuteronomy 21:21 as a charter for revenge! Yet the oft-quoted appeal for "an eye for an eye, a tooth for a tooth" has never been understood in Judaism "as a warrant for the extraction of vengeance", as one author points out. Rather, Jews see the text "as *limiting* retribution for injuries received, the limits to be determined by a court."[31]

Bearing in mind the ease with which one can misrepresent rival accounts of justice, we turn to the eastern faiths, and ask: is justice considered a virtue in Buddhism or Confucianism? And if so, does it condone the use of force?

Confucius typically answered the question indirectly, admitting a place for the administration of justice but preferring not to discuss it. Conflict, he said, should be resolved by arbitration rather than adjudication. If there was a rupture in a human relationship, the first port of call should be a healer, or a mediator, not a judge. "In hearing litigation, I am no different from any other man," he remarked. "But if you insist on a difference, it is, perhaps, that I try to get the parties not to resort to litigation in the first place."[32]

Himself abhorrent of war, Confucius came close to endorsing pacifism as the proper response to injustice. He said: "A resolute scholar and a man of humanity will never seek to live at the expense of injuring humanity. He would rather sacrifice his life in order to realise humanity."[33] When pressed on the subject, however, Confucius rejected the principle of "turning the other cheek". In the *Analects*, it is recorded:

> Someone said, "What do you think of repaying hatred with virtue?" Confucius said, "In that case what are you going to repay virtue with? Rather, repay hatred with uprightness and repay virtue with virtue."[34]

Not for the first time, we find Confucianism erring on the side of moderation in matters ethical. Buddhism, in contrast, is happier to celebrate pacifism. A famous episode from the *Jakata Stories* recalls:

The King of Benares and the King of Kosala met on a road. The path was too narrow for them both to proceed at once. Thus, it was agreed that most righteous king should pass first. The charioteer of the King of Kosala began listing his master's virtues thus:

"The strong he overthrows by strength. The mild by mildness. The good he conquers by goodness, And the wicked by wickedness too. Such is the nature of this king! Move out of the way, O charioteer!"

But the charioteer of the King of Benares was not impressed.

"If these are his *virtues*, what are his *faults*?" And he began to recite the virtues of the King of Benares.

"Anger he conquers by calmness, And by goodness the wicked. The stingy he conquers by gifts, And by truth the speaker of lies. Such is the nature of *this* king! Move out of the way, O charioteer!"

And when the King of Kosala heard this, he and his charioteer came down from their chariot and made way for the King of Benares.[35]

The Buddha himself rarely mentioned the word "justice", suggesting people should instead concentrate on enduring any wrongdoing that was perpetrated against them. Wrongdoers were not to be judged, moreover, but sympathetically understood, as the following religious story from India advises:

A scorpion had fallen into the water and the man reached in to rescue it from drowning. The scorpion immediately stung him, causing him to drop it again into the water. The man reached out again and again to rescue the scorpion and each time it stung him, causing him to drop it. A curious onlooker asked why he persisted. His response was "The scorpion's *dharm*

[nature] is to sting, my *dharm* as a human is compassion. How can I forgo my *dharm* and return injury for
injury, when even the scorpion is not willing to leave
his own?"[36]

In Zen Buddhism, such non-judgementalism is taken to extremes. Consider, for instance, the renowned Vietnamese
peace activist and Zen master Thich Nhat Hanh who wrote
the following response to the brutal beating in March 1991 of
Rodney King by officers of the Los Angeles Police Department:

> I was able to see that the policemen who were beat-
> ing Rodney King were also myself. . . . I am to blame;
> and I am responsible. . . . From the Buddhist perspec-
> tive, I have not practised deeply enough to transform
> the situation with the policemen. I have allowed vio-
> lence and misunderstanding to exist. . . . We are not
> observers. We are participants.[37]

Some will see an inherent danger with Nhat Hanh's view. After all, the language of "collective responsibility" is also spoken by terrorists — only they regard collective guilt as justification for global punishment, rather than global forgiveness.
But, in advocating something close to the latter, Nhat Hanh
does not reject the notion of personal responsibility. Nor
does he place an absolute ban on the use of force in the pursuit of justice. If someone is a danger to society, he writes:

> We are urged to act right away, put him in a situation
> where he cannot continue to harm people, even to
> lock him into a prison cell; we have to do that. But
> we have to do that with wisdom and compassion.[38]

Ultimately, Nhat Hanh argues not for the suspension of justice but for the administration of a sympathetic form of justice that contains "patience, understanding and tolerance". This is in keeping with the Buddha's social teaching, which has been characterised as "not an absolute pacifism, but a philosophical ethic, making for peace, moderation and magnanimity".[39] "All warfare in which man tries to slay his brother is lamentable," writes one religious scholar. But the Buddha "does not teach that those who go to war in a righteous cause after having exhausted all means to preserve the peace are blameworthy. He must be blamed who is the cause of war."[40]

Hinduism, likewise, rejects absolute pacifism on grounds of practicality. "No person in this world . . . can support life without injuring other creatures," says the *Mahabharata*. "The very ascetic leading a solitary life in the depths of the forest is no exception."[41] Gandhi similarly observed: "The very fact of his [man's] living — eating, drinking and moving about — necessarily involves some *himsa* [violence], destruction of life, be it ever so minute."[42] In such a manner, the Hindu politician defended his decision to support Britain in the First World War:

> I had hoped to improve my status and that of my people through the British Empire. Whilst in England I was enjoying the protection of the British Fleet, and taking shelter as I did under its armed might, I was directly participating in its potential violence. Therefore, if I desired to retain my connection with the Empire and to live under its banner, one of three courses was open to me: I could declare open resistance to the war and, in accordance with the law of *Satyagraha* [non-violent resistance], boycott the Empire until it

> changed its military policy; or I could seek imprison-
> ment by civil disobedience of such of its laws as were
> fit to be disobeyed; or I could participate in the war
> on the side of the Empire and thereby acquire the ca-
> pacity and fitness for resisting the violence of war. I
> lacked this capacity and fitness, so I thought there was
> nothing for it but to serve in the war.[43]

The logic might seem convoluted. But Gandhi saw no contradiction between his stance on the war and his support for
ahimsa, or non-violence. Like Nhat Hanh, Gandhi advocated
the suspension of not justice but judgementalism. Recalling
the discrimination he confronted in South Africa, where
white barbers refused to cut his hair, he said "the conviction
that it was punishment for our own sins saved me from becoming angry". Instead of looking outwards for someone to
blame he looked internally and realised "we [Hindus] do not
allow our barbers to serve our untouchable brethren".[44]

For Gandhi, the philosophical grounds for *satyagraha*, or
non-violent resistance, stemmed from the *Bhagavad-Gita*,
what might seem a strange source of justification. After all,
the treasured Hindu narrative centres on the story of Arjuna,
the warrior prince, who is persuaded by the god Krishna to
engage in a war against his enemies. Initially, Arjuna did not
want to fight, believing it to be better to die "unresisting and
unarmed" than to "kill our own people". Krishna made him
think otherwise, however, pointing out, among other things,
that those killed on the battle field would live on thanks to
reincarnation. "Never was there a time when I was not, nor
thou, nor these lords of men, nor will there ever be a time
hereafter when we shall cease to be," said Krishna.[45]

Ultimately, Arjuna accepted the argument that war was justified if certain conditions were met: the war had to be in a just
cause, and one had to engage in it without consideration for
one's personal well-being. Explaining his understanding of the
text, Gandhi wrote:

> I do not agree that the *Gita* advocates and teaches
> violence in any part of it. . . . Many of us make the
> very serious mistake of taking literally what is ac-
> cepted as scriptures. . . [The *Gita*] is pre-eminently a
> description of the duel that goes on in our own
> hearts. . . . It deals with the eternal duel between
> good and evil. . . . If it is difficult to reconcile certain
> verses with the teaching of non-violence, it is far
> more difficult to set the whole of the *Gita* in the
> framework of violence.[46]

What then can we say about justice as understood by the
world's great faiths, or more precisely justice in the context
of human conflict? Like all virtues, it lies between two vices,
those of moral indifference to wrongdoing, and knee-jerk
judgementalism. It may involve the use of force but only when
such force is administered cautiously and with restraint,
when, for instance, Islamic or Christian "just war" criteria are
met, or when punishment is informed by the "compassion
and understanding" of Zen Buddhism.

Critically, however, each faith acknowledges that there
are occasions when people should put their rightful griev-
ances to one side and forgive, tolerate, or simply understand
(this issue is teased out further in the next chapter). Buddhism encourages us to quell our sense of righteous indignation often. Confucianism not as frequently. But all faiths

declare at one time or another that justice — in the sense of demanding what is right and fair — should yield under certain circumstances to other virtues — virtues like mercy, tolerance and love. Even a faith so synonymous with justice as Islam concedes the point, as the following pair of historical tales illustrates:

> Caliph Omar was once faced with sentencing a Persian general named Harmuzan who had fought tirelessly against Islam. Harmuzan admitted that his execution would be just punishment for his crime.
>
> "I am ready to die," he told the Caliph. "But, first, could I have a drink of water? I am very thirsty."
>
> Omar told a servant to give a cup of water to the prisoner. Harmuzan said, "O! Caliph, I am afraid that I shall be killed while I am drinking this water!"
>
> The Caliph said, "I give you my word that you shall not be killed before you have drunk the water."
>
> Harmuzan laughed, "O! Caliph, you have promised that I shall not be killed before I drink this water!" He threw the cup on the ground. "Now I shall never drink this water and so you cannot kill me!"
>
> The Caliph smiled. 'You have tricked me, but I gave my promise. Go, you are free!'[47]

***

> Once, in a battle, Ali found himself face to face with an enemy soldier. The two men at once began to fight each other with their swords. After a while, the sword of the enemy soldier broke into two pieces. Ali at once lowered his sword for he would not kill a helpless enemy.
>
> The soldier said, "I shall not run away. Let me get a new sword and then I will fight you!" Ali held out

his own sword to his enemy. The soldier looked at
the sword and said, "Ali, you are indeed a brave man.
Why do you give your own sword to me?"

Ali replied, "When any man asks me for something, I give it to him."[48]

By any account the actions of Omar and Ali are irrational.
They comply with no theory of justice in western philosophy.
For secular theorists from Aristotle to Rawls, justice is the last
word on morality. No other virtue can trump it because, as
Aristotle said, "in justice is summed up the whole of virtue". It
is plainly irrational to say that something is just, and therefore
must be done, while recommending an alternative course of
action. Irrational, yes. But perhaps not immoral.

Who is to say that adhering to the demands of justice is
the best way of tackling human conflict? Take for example,
the conflict in Northern Ireland where major hostilities
ended only after the different factions dropped their competing claims for justice and asserted other virtues instead —
virtues like tolerance, wisdom and hope. A turning point for
many in the conflict was the reaction of Gordon Wilson to the
killing of his daughter, Marie, in the 1987 IRA bombing of En-
niskillen. Wilson — a soft-spoken Methodist who was subsequently drawn into peace and reconciliation work — was
door-stepped by reporters just hours after the bombing, and in
a voice charged with emotion made this incredible, irrational
but enormously powerful statement:

My wife, Joan, and I don't bear any grudges. We don't
feel any ill-will towards those who were responsible
for this. We see it as God's plan even though we might

> not understand it. I shall pray for those people [the
> bombers] tonight and every night.[49]

Religion may well be blamed for many of the world's conflicts. But here is an uncomfortable thought for rationalists: religion is perhaps better equipped than secular philosophy to resolve conflict — exactly because it has the capacity for abandoning reason and making justice subordinate to other virtues. For Wilson, as for Omar, Ali, Gandhi, and all us who are participants in the world's unfolding morality tale, there were — and there remain — no assurances. There is no guarantee that criminals will see the error of their ways if they are shown mercy. There is no guarantee that compassion will bring about an end to war. The awful, unsatisfactory truth is that we will never know if we were right to make justice subordinate to the demands of another virtue until after the event. But is that a reason not to try?

The world's great faiths answer in the negative. As Gandhi said, "a votary of truth is often obliged to grope in the dark".[50]

Endnotes

[1] Adapted from Bushnaq I. (1986), *Arab Folktales*, London & New York: Penguin Books, pp. 293–4.

[2] Hadith translated by Hamdard National Foundation, Pakistan.

[3] Ruthven, M. (2000), *Islam in the World*, New York: Oxford University Press, p. 219.

[4] Knappert, J. (1985), *Islamic Legends* (Vol I), The Netherlands: E.J. Brill, pp. 253–6.

[5] Knappert, J., *op. cit.*, p. 256.

[6] Matthew 5: 38–48.

7 Knappert, J., op. cit., p. 173.

8 Knappert, J., op. cit., pp. 173–4.

9 Khalidi, T. (2001), The Muslim Jesus, Sayings and Stories in Islamic Literature, Cambridge, Massachusetts: Harvard University Press, pp. 88–9.

10 Tolstoy's "What I Believe" as quoted in A.N. Wilson (ed.) (1987), The Lion and the Honeycomb: The Religious Writings of Tolstoy, translated by Robert Chandler. London: Collins, p. 37.

11 "The Kingdom of God is Within You", as quoted in A.N. Wilson (ed.) op. cit., pp. 79–80.

12 Qur'an 17:33 as quoted in Nicholson R.A. (1969), A Literary History of the Arabs, Cambridge University Press, p. 91.

13 Norris, H.T. (1980), The Adventures of Antar (Approaches to Arab Literature, No. 3), Wilts, England: Aris & Phillips Ltd, p. 210.

14 Norris, H.T., op. cit., p. 215.

15 Assad Nimer Busool (1993), Good Neighbours and Other Moral Stories, Chicago: IQRA' International Educational Foundation, p. 41.

16 The Qur'an 22:39.

17 Williams, J. A., "Misunderstanding Islam" as cited at www.israelshamir.net.

18 Fashing, D.J. and Dechant, D. (2001), Comparative Religious Ethics, Massachusetts: Blackwell, pp. 257–8.

19 Qur'an 17:33.

20 Qur'an 22:39.

21 Qur'an 2:190.

22 Qur'an 5:32.

23 Dorff, E.N. (2003), "A Jewish Perspective on Human Rights'" in J. Runzo, N.M. Martin and A. Sharma (eds.), Human Rights and Responsibilities in the World Religions, Oxford: Oneworld, p. 211.

24 Deuteronomy 20: 10-14.

25 Broyde, M.J. (2003), "Fighting the War and the Peace: Battlefield Ethics, Peace Talks, Treaties, and Pacifism in the Jewish Tradition", Jewish Law Articles: www.jlaw.com.

26 Qur'an 8:61.

27 Qur'an 23:96.

28 Qur'an 60:7.

29 Matthew 7:1.

[30] Dietrich Bonhoeffer, "The Cost of Discipleship", as cited in J. Runzo and N.M. Martin (eds.), *Ethics in the World Religions*, Oxford: Oneworld, p. 329.

[31] O'Sullivan, O. (2002), *One God, Three Faiths*, Dublin: Columba, p. 10.

[32] Lun Yu 12:13 as cited in Cua A.S. (1998), *Moral Vision and Tradition: Essays in Chinese Ethics*, Catholic University of America Press: Washington DC, p. 311.

[33] *The Analects* 15:8.

[34] *The Analects* 14:36.

[35] Adapted from Rhys-Davids, C.A.F. (1998), *Buddhist Birth-Stories*, New Delhi: Srishti Publishers and Distributors, pp. xxiv–xxv.

[36] Madhu Kishwar, "In Defense of our Dharma" as cited in J. Runzo, N.M. Martin and A. Sharma (eds.), *op. cit.*, pp. 270–1.

[37] Nhat Hanh, T., "We Are the Beaters; We Are the Beaten", *Los Angeles Times*, 15 April 1991.

[38] Nhat Hanh, T., "Dharma Talk" in *Plum Village* on 28 July 1996 as cited at www.plumvillage.org.

[39] Norman Bentwich, "The Religious Foundations of Internationalism", as cited in J. Runzo, N.M. Martin and A. Sharma (eds.), *op cit.*, p. 105.

[40] Paul Carus, "The Gospel of Buddha" as cited in J. Runzo, N.M. Martin and A. Sharma (eds.), *op. cit.*, p. 105.

[41] Radhakrishnan S. and Moore C.A. (eds.) (1957), *A Sourcebook in Indian Philosophy*, New Jersey: Princeton University Press, p. 166.

[42] Gandhi, M.K. (1927), *An Autobiography*, Ahmedabad, India: Navajivan Trust, p. 291.

[43] Gandhi, M.K., *op. cit.*, p. 292.

[44] Gandhi, M.K., *op. cit.*, p. 179.

[45] Radhakrishnan S. and Moore C.A. (eds.), *op. cit.*, pp. 101–63.

[46] Gandhi, "The Teaching of the Gita", as cited in Fashing, D.J. and Dechant, D., *op. cit.*, p. 127.

[47] Adapted from Whyte, R. (1966), *Ten Stories from Islam*, Lahore: Pakistan Branch, Oxford University Press, pp. 31–2.

[48] Whyte, R., *op. cit.*, p. 39.

[49] BBC interview as reported in *The Irish Times*, 9 November 1987.

[50] Gandhi, M.K., *op. cit.*, p. 291.

14

MERCY

'Umar Ibn 'Abd al-'Aziz (a "righteous caliph", and
follower of Islam, who lived in the first century after
the death of Muhammad) ordered punishment for a
man in his absence. He vowed to punish him severely,
if Allah helped him capture the man. 'Umar succeeded
in capturing the man, and he proceeded to punish
him. Raja' Ibn Haywah, his minister, said to him:

"Allah already did for you what you wished the
most. Now you do what Allah likes the most — forgive."

Hearing this, 'Umar forgave the man and allowed
him to go free.[1]

This chapter should be read in tandem with the last, because
mercy and justice are inextricably linked, or perhaps more
precisely in direct contrast to one another. After all, how can
you value both justice and mercy at once when you face
someone guilty of wrongdoing? Surely you must either forgive

or punish and, if so, how do you decide which? A convenient answer is that mercy should be shown to those who apologise for wrongdoing, and justice for those who don't. Convenient — but not an answer any of the world's major faiths give. Sure, repentance is celebrated in Christian parables like that of *The Prodigal Son*.[2] But nowhere does Jesus say mercy is conditional on repentance. Far from it, as we shall read later. In Islam, meanwhile, it is obligatory for a Muslim to accept the apology of a fellow Muslim. But nowhere is it stated that one should *only* forgive when an apology is made. As the story above suggests, mercy can — and should — be performed on no other grounds than because "it pleases Allah".

Another convenient answer to the question above is that mercy is simply a form of justice. The US-based Islamic scholar Khaled Abou El Fadl suggests this when he writes:

> In the Qur'anic discourse, mercy is not simply forgiveness or the willingness to ignore the faults and sins of people. Mercy is a state in which the individual is able to be just with himself or herself and with others by giving each their due. Fundamentally, mercy is tied to a state of true and genuine perception . . .[3]

To describe mercy as justice, however, one must define justice as somehow "divine", or of a higher order to the virtue that we examined in the previous chapter. For instance, one could say, "ordinary" justice demands what is right and fair but "divine" justice demands otherwise — specifically the conquering of "ordinary" justice with mercy. But is this not just another way of saying, "Justice (the virtue we examined in the previous chapter) should sometimes yield to other virtues, mercy included"?

We will return to this question — the question of how to value, or deal with, competing virtues — in the Epilogue. Some clue to an answer, however, may be drawn from an examination of mercy, as a virtue in its own right, in the world's major religions.

In Islam, mercy is as celebrated as justice, if not more so, in scripture and stories. In fact, there is a case for saying mercy, rather than justice, is Islam's defining virtue.

Perhaps no military leader is better associated with mercy in the western world than Saladin, who led a Muslim army against the third Christian Crusade of the Middle Ages. When he recaptured Jerusalem from the Christians in 1187, Saladin entered a city that had once been painted with the blood of Muslims. The city's sacred mosque had been used as a stable for horses, and the rock from which Muhammad was believed to have ascended to heaven had been vandalised. Yet Saladin ordered his soldiers to take no revenge. A token ransom was arranged for Christian captives, many of whom Saladin freed with his own money. The defeated Crusaders responded to this gesture by smuggling gold and treasure out of the city rather than use it to free others Christians.

Such mercy as that shown by Saladin was unheard of in a conflict as bloody as the Crusades. But, then, Saladin was merely following the example of Muhammad when the Prophet captured Mecca. According to the Qur'an, Muhammad's defeated enemies had tormented him for 11 years but the Prophet announced that he would behave with them the way Yusuf had behaved with his cruel brothers saying: ". . . This day let no reproach be [cast] on you: Allah will forgive you, and He is the Most Merciful of those who show mercy!"[4]

The episode to which Muhammad referred exists in the Judeo-Christian tradition too but arguably not with the same prominence. The Qur'an describes it as "the best of stories", or the "most beautiful of stories".[5] It recounts how Yusuf (Joseph) was betrayed by his jealous brothers but came to forgive them after enduring many painful years in exile. The brothers had beaten Yusuf to near-death and had him tossed into a desert well where he was found by a passing Bedouin warrior who made him his slave. Some time later, Yusuf was wrongly accused of seducing the wife of the king of Egypt, and thrown into jail for 12 years. He eventually found favour with the king after offering him some useful advice. Yusuf was then appointed vizier when he was one day called to meet a group of travellers in search of food: it was Yusuf's cruel brothers, who had fallen on hard times. Instead of punishing them, Yusuf sent them home with bags full of riches. "I am the one who was lost, and I have forgiven you," he exclaimed, before a happy reunification with his father Jacob.[6]

In Christianity, mercy is likewise hailed, most famously in the Biblical episode of *The Woman Caught in Adultery*. In John's Gospel, we hear of Jesus telling those who planned to stone an adulteress to death: "Let him who is without sin among you be the first to throw a stone at her." The story continues:

> Jesus was left alone with the woman standing before him. He looked up and said to her, "Woman, where are they? Has no one condemned you?"
>
> She said, "No one, Lord." And Jesus said, "Neither do I condemn you; go, and do not sin again."[7]

Jesus portrayed forgiveness as a means of atoning for sin. The more we forgave, the more God would forgive us. Or, as said in the *Lord's Prayer*, "Forgive us our trespasses, as we forgive those who trespass against us."[8] Jesus elaborated on the theme in Matthew's Gospel, saying God would punish "every one of you if you do not forgive your brother from your heart". It is said:

> Peter came up and said to him, "Lord, how often shall my brother sin against me, and I forgive him? As many as seven times?" Jesus said to him, "I do not say to you seven times, but seventy times seven."[9]

Jesus regarded only one sin to be unforgivable, and that was "blasphemy against the Holy Spirit". He said:

> He who is not with me is against me, and he who does not gather with me scatters. Therefore I tell you, every sin and blasphemy will be forgiven, but the blasphemy against the Spirit will not be forgiven. And whoever says a word against the Son of Man will be forgiven; but whoever speaks against the Holy Spirit will not be forgiven, either in this age or in the age to come.[10]

For Muslims, apostasy is one of three "unforgivable" sins, according to conventional Islamic teaching. The other two such sins, which — in accordance with certain *hadiths* — are also supposed to carry the death penalty, are murder and adultery. The Qur'an seems to be a little more lenient on the latter, proscribing a hundred lashes for the "the woman and the man guilty of adultery or fornication". It says: "Let not compassion move you in their case, in a matter prescribed by

Allah, if ye believe in Allah and the Last Day: and let a party of the Believers witness their punishment."[11]

As for apostasy, the Qur'an is not as clear-cut as conservative Muslims would like to think. It states:

> It is part of the Mercy of Allah that thou dost deal gently with them [unbelievers]. Wert thou severe or harsh-hearted, they would have broken away from about thee: so pass over [their faults], and ask for [Allah's] forgiveness for them; and consult them in affairs [of moment]. Then, when thou hast taken a decision, put thy trust in Allah. For Allah loves those who put their trust [in Him].[12]

Some Muslim scholars argue that apostasy can only be forgiven if the guilty party apologises for his or her sins, and returns to Islam. However, one must ask: is such a mean-spirited, if not cruel, response to free thought in keeping with the example of Muhammad? According to a frequently told legend, the Prophet once visited Taif to spread the word of Allah but instead was pelted with stones and run out of the city. On taking shelter, he was visited by an angel who was on his way to Taif to destroy its people for their sin of mistreating Muhammad. But the Prophet prayed to Allah, urging Him to save the people. "Guide these people, because they did not know what they were doing," he said, his words echoing those of Jesus on the Cross: "Father, forgive them; for they know not what they do."[13]

But what of the attitude of eastern faiths to mercy? In Hinduism and Buddhism, the virtue is closely associated with self-discipline. The vengeful lose their temper, or lose control of themselves, and suffer as much as, if not more than, the victims of their wrath. Exemplars of mercy can be found throughout Hindu lore, in characters like Drona and Nala, who not only forgave their enemies but rewarded them with half their wealth. Perhaps the supreme practitioner of mercy, however, was Yudhishthira, who in the Hindu epic of the *Mahabharata* forbade vengeance against those who tricked him out of his kingdom. Wandering in the wilderness without a penny to his name, he was challenged by his wife Draupadi. "A man should act," she said, "lest by inaction he is censured". Describing the unjust manner in which their foe, Duryodhana, stole their wealth, she asked:

> Can I praise your god who permits such inequality? What reward does your god receive when it allows Duryodhana to prosper — he who is full of evil; he who destroys virtue and religion? If sin does not rebound on the sinner, then a man's might is the greatest force and not your god, and I sorrow for those who are devoid of might.

The semi-divine Bhima supported her pleadings for retaliation, charging Yudhishthira with weakness. "O thou art like froth," he cried. "Thou art unripe fruit! O king, strike down your enemies! Battle is the highest virtue for a Kshatriya [a member of the reigning order]." Yudhishthira replied with one the most eloquent tributes to mercy to be found in any faith:

> Anger is sinful; it is the cause of destruction. He who is angry cannot distinguish between right and wrong. Anger slays one who should be revered; it reveres one who should be slain. An angry man may commit his own soul to hell. Know you that wise men control their wrath so as to achieve prosperity both in this

world and in the next. A weak man cannot control his
wrath; but men of wisdom and insight seek to subdue
their passions, knowing that he who is angry cannot
perceive things in their true perspective. None but ignorant people regard anger as equivalent to energy. . .
. If wrongs were not righted except by chastisement,
the whole world would speedily be destroyed, for anger is destruction; it makes men slay one another. O
fair Draupadi! . . . one should forgive every wrong. He
who is forgiving shall attain to eternal bliss; he who is
foolish and cannot forgive is destroyed both in this
world and in the next. Forgiveness is the greatest virtue; it is sacrifice; it is tradition; it is inspiration. Forgiveness, O beautiful one! is holiness; it is Truth; it is
Brahma [the highest god]. By forgiveness the universe
is made steadfast . . .[14]

Mercy is also a key virtue in Confucianism. To Confucius, superior governments ruled by positive examples of virtue,
rather than by negative schemes of law enforcement, or punishment. However, according to Confucian thought, unrestrained mercy can be just as harmful as unrestrained vengeance. This message is reinforced in moral stories which tell of
people "spoiled" by leniency. One such tale from Chinese lore
recounts how a criminal who was sentenced to death bit off
one of his mother's nipples, blaming her for the fact that he
had ended up in the predicament. The story has its equivalent
in *Aesop's Fables*, only it is an ear of the criminal's mother that
gets bitten off instead.[15] The commentary with the tale goes:
"Nip evil in the bud. Spare the rod and spoil the child." Such
stories may seem harsh, if not barbaric, today but they rein-
force two related beliefs in religious traditions: First, being
punished, or doing penance for your sins, can be to your own

benefit. Had the mother in the tale above imposed some limits on her son's behaviour, for example, he might have been spared the final lesson of execution. The second lesson to be drawn from such stories is that every crime has extenuating circumstances. The latter is perhaps the key to appreciating mercy — for unless we try to understand why someone performed a wrongful act we will never forgive him or her.

Mercy, so understood, is predicated on the notion that everyone has some good in them, or, as the saying goes, "Even a stopped clock tells the right time twice a day". A sure-fire way of withholding mercy is to deny that wrongdoers are capable of goodness. More effective still is to deny that they are human.

One doesn't need to delve deep into history to discover examples of people taking the latter course. The cheerleaders for the 1994 Rwandan genocide, for instance, described the fleeing Tutsis as cockroaches (*inyenzi*), presumably so the *genocidaires* would find it easier to kill them off. Consistent with such thinking was the eighth, and most often quoted, of the "Hutu Ten Commandments", namely: "Hutus must stop having mercy on the Tutsis".

On a more basic level, people withhold mercy by closing their minds to an explanation for wrongdoing. Take, for example, the trial of the two ten-year-old boys charged with murdering the Liverpool infant James Bulger. In the wake of the killing, the then British prime minister John Major declared: "We must condemn a little more, and understand a little less." The author Blake Morrison picked up on the comment in his book *As If*, remarking:

Only a culture without hope cannot forgive — a culture that doesn't believe in progress or redemption.
Have we so little faith in ourselves we can't accept the
possibility of maturation, change, cure?[16]

To understand is to forgive. The saying is well appreciated in
all faiths. A final morality tale from Chinese lore tells of an
ancient ruler Lord Mengchang, who made a blacklist of 500
men who had abandoned him while he was temporarily out
of office. His sagacious advisor Feng Huan told him not to
harbour any bitterness, however, explaining:

"Have you noticed the shoppers in the marketplace? In the morning they push and jostle to shove
their way into the marketplace. But when it gets dark,
they turn away from the place. They don't even look
back. Not that they like it less in the evening than they
like it in the morning, but what they want is not there
in the evening. When you lost your position, your
guests simply went away for the same reason — they
couldn't get what they wanted. There is no need for
you to bear grudge against them. I hope you will treat
them exactly as you did in the past."

Lord Mengchang bowed . . . took his advice and
had the names of the five hundred men that he had
blacklisted scraped from his record.[17]

Endnotes

[1] Assad Nimer Busool (1993), *Good Neighbours and Other Moral Stories*,
Chicago: IQRA' International Educational Foundation, p. 5.
[2] Luke 15:11–32.

3 Abou El-Fadl, K. (2003), "The Human Rights Commitment in Modern Islam" in J. Runzo, N.M. Martin and A. Sharma (eds.), *Human Rights and Responsibilities in the World Religions*, Oxford: Oneworld, p. 330.

4 Qur'an 12: 92.

5 Qur'an 12:3.

6 Knappert, J. (1985), *Islamic Legends*, The Netherlands: E.J. Brill, p. 102.

7 John 8: 2–11

8 Matthew 6:9–13.

9 Matthew 18:21–35.

10 Matthew 12:30.

11 Qur'an 24:2.

12 Qur'an 3:159.

13 Luke 23:34.

14 Mackenzie D.A. (1913), *Indian Myth and Legend*, London: Gresham Publishing, pp. 252–3.

15 Rhys, E. (ed.) (1928), *Aesop's Fables*, London: J.M. Dent & Sons, p. 48.

16 Morrison, B. (1997), *As If*, London: Granta, pp. 239–40.

17 Tang, C. (1996), *A Treasury of China's Wisdom*, Beijing: Foreign Languages Press, p. 185.

EPILOGUE

"How should I live?" That was the question posed at the outset of this book. What answer have we got from the world's major religious traditions? Not a simple one, that's for sure. Each tradition tells its own story of virtue, celebrating a variety of human endeavours. But at the heart of these disparate tales, is there a single narrative which can be read as a guide for living?

If so, it must praise a combination of virtues. One thing on which all traditions agree is that you should not concentrate on any one single virtue to the detriment of all others. That goes even for love, which you cannot practice to the extreme without denying value in your own life. It would seem, therefore, that any protagonist in a story of virtue that is universal to all traditions would need a sense of balance. He or she would need to have a number of qualities, and not just one redeeming feature. He or she would need, among other things, the empathy of a Buddha, the compassion of a Good Samaritan, the industry of a Mencius, the mercy of a Muhammad, the honesty of a Simeon Ben Shetach, and the tolerance of a Ghandi. Not an easy character to imagine, let alone emulate.

But perhaps we can imagine the sort of values he or she would endorse. Consider the following proposition: that underpinning the world's major religious traditions is a shared view on how people should — in a very fundamental way — interact with one another. Consider, specifically, the possibility of Christians, Muslims, Buddhists, Jews, Confucians, Hindis, Humanists, and so on, agreeing upon a statement of moral intent — call it *A Universal Declaration of Virtue*. It is a bold suggestion but, then, as Abraham taught his followers, audacity is no bad thing.

What would such a Declaration look like? Well, as its name suggests, it might be modelled on the Universal Declaration of Human Rights (UDHR) in the sense of setting an ethical standard for all of humanity. But unlike the UDHR, to which governments are asked to commit themselves, a Universal Declaration of Virtue might be something in the first instance for someone like you or I.[1] It might, in brief, look something like this:

A Universal Declaration of Virtue

Acknowledging that no one is perfect but that this shouldn't stop me from seeking perfection;

Acknowledging that there is some value in everyone;

Acknowledging that I have a social responsibility to improve myself;

I commit myself:

To be human, and in the face of suffering let myself cry (*Empathy*);

To consider others as myself, and to treat them as I would wish them to treat me (*Compassion*);

Not to ask but to give (*Charity*);

To avoid extremes, control my temper, and sometimes be silent (*Self-discipline*);

To be faithful to my family, community or friends but, above all, to my convictions (*Loyalty*);

To keep the faith while questioning it (*Audacity*);

To tell the truth for its own sake, while accepting there is such a thing as a noble lie (*Honesty*);

To never boast or think too highly of myself, remembering "pride before a fall" (*Humility*);

To look for the good, rather than the bad, in other people and in other people's beliefs (*Tolerance*);

To accept the truth from whichever source it comes, and apply perspective in the case of good fortune or ill, knowing "this too shall pass" (*Wisdom*);

Not to waste my time, nor my talents (*Work*);

To put myself last and my beloved first; to surrender to something greater than me (*Love*);

To be slow to judge others, and try to make peace rather than war (*Justice*);

To try to understand why people do wrong, and forgive whether or not I get an apology (*Mercy*).

The Declaration may be audacious in character but it is offered in a spirit of humility. It aims not to be the last word on religious ethics but rather the first word in a dialogue between the traditions. For a start, some readers may question its selectivity. The fourteen virtues discussed in this book and summarised above were chosen to try to ensure all the major religious traditions were covered more or less equally. But some readers may feel certain traditions are better represented than others, and to redress the imbalance a shorter, or perhaps longer, list is required. A strong case, for instance, could be made for the inclusion of Gratitude, a key virtue of Buddhism; or Cleanliness, a virtue of similar stature in Islam; or Hope, a hallmark of Protestant ethics and related moral philosophies. Similarly, a case could be made for the virtue described by Aristotle as "most necessary for living", namely Friendship (although it is part-covered by Loyalty).[2] Or a case could be made for Politeness, described by the writer and philosopher Andre Comte-Sponville as "the first virtue and the origin perhaps of all others".[3] A case could also be made for many of the 52 core virtues identified by The Virtues Project, a US-based educational organisation which incidentally doesn't include Empathy on its list but does include virtues like Creativity, Enthusiasm, Orderliness, Reliability and Tact.[4]

That none of these virtues has been included in the Declaration of Virtue above is not to bar them from being classified as *universal*. Nor is it to denigrate their importance within their respective faiths. After all, such a Declaration is not a substitute for religious belief but a complementary statement consistent with that belief. Call it a prayer, if you like, for like a prayer it can be said in tandem with religious, or secular, worship. A Muslim might assert the same, or similar, principles to those above in the name of Allah, a Christian in the name of Jesus Christ, and a secular humanist in the name of "our shared humanity". Each would recite the "prayer" for different reasons. But does it really matter? Surely, what matters most is that everyone tries to meet the ideals contained therein.

The Nobel Prize-winning physicist Richard P. Feynman was certainly of this view, citing bitter arguments within Christianity over whether Jesus was of a substance *like* the Father or of the *same* substance *as* the Father. "Reputations were destroyed, people were killed, arguing whether it's the same or similar. And today we should learn that lesson and not have an argument as to the reason *why* we agree if we agree." That agreement was possible "on consequences, . . . on the net result" was all too evident to Feynman in his own life even if, he said, agreement was impossible "on the reason we do what we ought to do". For instance, the physicist said he shared the views of Pope John XXIII in his encyclical on the duties and responsibilities of mankind even though "I do not agree with some of the machinery which supports some of the ideas, that they spring from God . . . or that some of these ideas are the natural consequence of ideas of earlier popes."[5]

If we accept that agreement is possible on a Universal Declaration of Virtue, however, what then? Can one apply the declaration to real-life scenarios in order to get answers to tricky moral questions? The philosopher Peter Singer suggests not, arguing: "If we are to achieve consensus on a common ethic, we are unlikely to be able to go beyond a few very broad principles. Hence, it may be said, these universally accepted ethical standards, if they exist at all, will not be the kind of thing that political leaders can draw on to show that they are justified in intervening in the affairs of another state."[6]

This criticism can be levelled against a Universal Declaration of Virtue. If the world's leaders were to sign up to such a

Declaration, would we be any closer to having a definitive ruling on, for instance, when and how one state is justified in waging war against another? In particular, there is a question over how to deal with virtues which clash with one another — virtues like faith and audacity, tolerance and loyalty, or charity and justice. Under certain circumstances, it is far from easy to establish which virtue should take precedence. If mercy means forgiving your enemies and justice means giving them a fair trial, what, for instance, should you do if you are victorious in war? Grant an amnesty to your defeated foes or prosecute them in court?

Governments tend to adjudicate on such matters on the basis of practical rather than moral considerations — on the basis, for example, of whether "demanding justice" after war will trigger a fresh conflict. But is there an alternative means of adjudicating between two, or more, competing virtues? Aristotle suggests there is when he writes that "intention is the decisive factor in virtue and character".[7] The argument runs that an action performed in the right spirit (or with the best of intentions) is good, even if the result it produces is bad.

The argument, however, will strike many as unsatisfactory. Indeed, it seems to hold as much water as the counter-argument that the decisive factor, in establishing whether an action is virtuous, is the consequence of the action rather than its motivation. Support for this counter-argument can be found in Dostoevsky's *A Nasty Story*, a tale of one man's misery brought about by another man's well-intentioned interference. In the story, a Russian army general calls in unannounced to the humble wedding of a junior officer, thinking it would do the man a great honour. In fact, the poor soldier is

devastated by the gesture as he feels obliged to ply the unin-
vited guest with champagne and other luxuries, borrowing
money in the process from the rest of the wedding party.
The general is unaware that his "good deed" leads to the
groom's financial ruin.[8]

An alternative means of adjudicating between the demands of rival virtues can be found in Buddhism. The faith
teaches that appreciating the right thing to do in a particular
set of circumstances cannot be learned from a book. Instead,
one must apply "skilful means", the nature of which becomes
clearer as enlightenment approaches. Mysterious as it may
sound, this form of moral adjudication sits well with the
thinking of other religious traditions. In each tradition, the
good person is like a juggler of different virtues. Sometimes
compassion is given priority, or released to the highest point
of the juggling cycle, sometimes justice, and so on. But,
throughout, all virtues are within the juggler's reach. It takes a
skilled juggler to keep several balls in the air at once, just as it
takes a good person to keep many virtues circulating in his or
her character in harmony.

"A sense of balance" might be another way of describing
this human quality. People who lack balance will as easily
chose vice over virtue, as demonstrated, for example, by religious fundamentalists who support acts of terrorism, believing such acts to be just.

Again, however, we are presented with the problem of
applicability. What criteria do we use to judge whether a
government or individual is "balanced" "juggling well", or "using skilful means", in presiding over moral dilemmas? There is
no easy answer, except for this: the worst type of character is

fixated on a single virtue — say, loyalty, or justice perhaps — to the neglect of all others, just as the poorest form of juggler can throw no more than a single ball up and down in the air.

Rationalists like Peter Singer see little value in imagining a universal faith-based ethic because of this question-mark over applicability. He predicts that any attempt at applying a no-tionally agreed moral framework will ultimately descend into a dispute about underlying religious belief.[9] His pessimism is perhaps well founded. But what is the alternative to imagining, and working towards, agreement between the world's major faiths? Allowing misunderstanding to fester, and to spill over into radical and violent confrontation? As the Catholic theolo-gian Hans Küng says: "No survival without a world ethic. No world peace without peace between religions. No peace be-tween the religions without dialogue between the religions."[10]

The notion of people from different faiths agreeing to a Universal Declaration of Virtue may seem like a remote pos-sibility; the idea of applying that Declaration in the real world perhaps more so. But, were it to happen, the prize would indeed be great. For religious believers, a Universal Declara-tion of Virtue would validate their moral standards in the eyes of non-believers. For secular moral agents, such a Decla-ration would have the benefit of making religious difference, at a fundamental level, irrelevant.

Modesty, perseverance and audacity are among the virtues we will have to call upon to achieve this goal — the goal of genuine inter-faith dialogue. It is a daunting task. But it is not an impossible one. And if you are looking for a way to start the exchange, you could do worse than tell someone a story.

Endnotes

1 It is worth noting that an alternative statement of moral intent, specifically for religious leaders, is already in circulation. The Parliament of the World's Religions commissioned the Catholic theologian Hans Küng to draft in 1992 a "Declaration of the Religions for a Global Ethic", which the parliament endorsed the following year. There has been little follow-up, however, to the publication of the 4,000-word declaration, which perhaps warrants revival today (See: www.cpwr.org).

2 VIII (i) in Thomson J.A.K. (translator) (1977), *The Nicomachean Ethics*, Middlesex, England: Penguin, p. 258.

3 Comte-Sponville, A. (2001), *A Short Treatise on the Great Virtues*, London: William Heinemann, p. 7.

4 See www.virtuesproject.com/virtueslist.html.

5 Feynman, R.P. (1999), *The Meaning of It All*, London: Penguin, pp. 121–2.

6 Singer, P. (2004), *One World* (second edition), New Haven & London: Yale University Press, pp. 142–3.

7 VIII (xiii) in Thomson J.A.K., *op. cit.*, p. 284.

8 Coulson J. (translates) (1966) Fyodor Dostoyevsky: *The Gambler/Bobok/A Nasty Story*, Middlesex, Penguin, pp. 185–238.

9 Singer, P., *op. cit.*, pp. 143-4.

10 Küng, H. (1991), *Global Responsibility: In Search of a New World Ethic*, London: SCM Press, p .xv.

INDEX

'Abd al-Jabbar, 176, 181
'Abd al-Malik, 212
Abraham, 93–5, 101
Abu Bakr, 81–3
Abu Yazid al-Bistami, 192
Adam, 20, 198
Adam and Eve, 5
Adham, 111–2
Aesop's Fables, 5, 50, 89, 124,
    182, 236
afterlife, 7
ahisma, 37
Ali, Ayaan Hirsi, 103
Allah, 76, 84, 128, 196, 234
Allen, Woody, 98
Al-Qaeda, 55, 83, 136
Ambedkar, Dr B.R., 41
Analects, 34, 47
Antar, 212
Apology for Idlers, 179
apostates, 40, 95, 103, 233
Apostles, 83
Aristotle, 8, 10, 24, 46, 102,
    205, 225, 244
Arjuna, 8, 48, 222

Arkoun, Mohammed, 103
Art of War, 115
asceticism, 69–70
atheists, 116
audacity, 2, 93–106
Augustine, 21–2, 33, 190,
    216
Averroes, 102

Beatitudes, 47
Bentham, Jeremy, 118
Berrigan, Father Daniel, 100
Bhagavad-Gita, 8, 48, 86, 222
Bharata, 62–3
Bible, 36, 49, 99, 101, 156,
    193; *see also under names*
    of Books
bodhisattvas, 61–2, 108
Bonhoeffer, Dietrich, 216
Bono, 42
Boy and the Nettle, 89
Boy Who Cried Wolf, 108, 120
Buddha, 14–15, 17, 23, 25–7,
    31, 36, 37, 60, 61, 63–4,
    108, 160–1, 162–3, 173,
    185–6, 194, 219, 221

Buddhism, 2, 3, 6, 23, 25–6,
  32, 36, 37, 60–1, 65, 73,
  108, 115, 144, 157, 162,
  174, 194, 247
Bulger, James, 237
Bush, George, 145

Catholic Church, 79, 80, 99,
  116, 146, 160
Catholicism, 33, 40
Ch'an, 61
charity, 45–58
Christianity, 2, 3, 6, 10, 18,
  30, 32, 36, 38, 55, 65,
  69–70, 79, 83, 99, 160,
  190–1, 206–11, 216–7
Chuang Tzu, 143, 156, 159
chung, 34
Churchill, Winston, 116
chutzpah, 94, 98
cleanliness, 244
compassion, 29–44
Comte-Sponville, Andre, 244
Confucianism, 3, 23, 33, 40,
  54, 65, 76, 130, 157, 174,
  195, 236
Confucius, 5, 18, 34–5, 46,
  47, 54, 64–5, 73, 76, 90,
  108, 115, 130, 159, 173,
  218, 236
creativity, 244
Crusades, 145, 231

Dante Alighieri, 192–3
Dawkins, Richard, 137
deontology, 8
Dershowitz, Alan, 137
de Spinoza, Benedict, 159

Discourse on the Moral Effects
  of the Arts and Sciences, 177
Divine Comedy, The, 192
Doctrine of the Mean, 35, 64,
  130, 144
Dostoevsky, 52, 246
Doubting Thomas, 80

Ebadi, Shirin, 104
Ecclesiastes, see Kohelet
El Fadl, Khaled Abou, 149,
  230
El-Ghazalli, Muhammad,
  148–9
empathy, 13–28
Encyclical on the Relationship
  between Faith and Reason,
  100
enthusiasm, 244
Epic of Gilgamesh, The, 16
Eucharist, 7

Fables of Bidpai, 109
faith, 81
Fatima, 20
Feng Huan, 238
Feynman, Richard P., 245
First Noble Truth, 26
Four Sights, The, 14–5, 26
free will, 32
friendship, 78, 244
fundamentalism, 6, 9

Gandhi, Mahatma, 9, 37–8,
  40, 56, 73, 77, 113–4, 130,
  138–40, 142, 180, 221–3,
  226
Garden of Eden, 39, 119

Garden of Gethsemane, 21, 100
Genesis, 116, 172
genocide, 97
Gibran, Kahlil, 189
God, 7, 32–3, 39, 48–9, 54–5, 70, 76, 78–9, 81, 94–7, 100–1, 116, 120, 127, 132–3, 135, 139, 146–8, 172, 189, 191–3, 196, 208, 214–15, 233
Goethe, 99
Golden Rule, 30, 33, 35–7, 41–3, 189, 204
Good Samaritan, 30–1
good works, 36, 46, 90
Graham, Franklin, 145
gratitude, 244
Gray, John, 87
Great Learning, The, 76
Greenberg, Irving, 97
Guinness, 89

Harris, Sam, 136–7, 142, 149
Heidegger, Martin, 26
Herschel, Abraham Joshua, 24
Hinduism, 3, 4, 6, 17, 37, 40, 48, 99, 115, 130, 158, 221
Hobbes, Thomas, 119
Holocaust, 96–7
homosexuality, 141–2
honesty, 107–22
honour killings, 127–8
hope, 244
Hsun Tzu, 77, 144
humility, 123–34
Hussein, 19

Hutus, 237

Idiot, The, 52
ijtihad, 101
Inquisition, 145
Isaac, 101
Ishmael, 101
Islam, 2, 3, 6, 10, 16, 38, 40, 51, 54, 65–70, 78, 90, 99, 101–2, 124–8, 148, 196–7, 206–15, 217
Israel, 96

Jacob, 20, 96
Jainism, 37, 137–8
Jakata Stories, 5, 37, 60, 160, 194, 218
jen, 18, 23, 34
Jesuits, 22
Jesus Christ, 4, 7, 20–1, 38, 52, 66–70, 73, 79, 80–1, 83, 90, 100, 132, 142, 146–7, 150, 160, 173, 189, 190–1, 197–8, 199, 205–9, 211, 216, 230, 232–3, 234, 244
jihad, 214
Job, 95
John's Gospel, 232
Joseph, 20, 231–2
Judaism, 2, 3, 30, 32, 66, 84, 94–8, 180, 191, 214–5, 217
justice, 2, 6, 203–28

Kabbalah, 193
Kadir, Abdul, 113
King, Martin Luther, 100
King, Rodney, 220
King Solomon, 124
Kohelet, 162

Krishna, 48, 222
Küng, Hans, 248

Laborem Exercens, 172
Lane, Edward, 125
Lao Tzu, 123, 131, 156, 179
Lazarus, 21
Levi-Yitzhak, Rabbi, 97
loyalty, 75–92
love, 2, 185–201
Lovelock, James E., 119
Loyola, Ignatius, 22
Luke's Gospel, 132, 146

MacIntyre, Alasdair, 8
Mahabharata, 4, 85, 115, 158, 166, 221, 235
Major, John, 237
Manji, Irshad, 104
Man with Two Wives, 151
Marmulak, 104
martyrdom, 84
Marx, Groucho, 98
Mathnawi, 139
Matthew's Gospel, 68, 181, 207, 216, 233
McGee, Seana, 187
Mencius, 18, 33, 144, 157, 174
Mengchang, Lord, 238
mercy, 229–39
Mesopotamia, 16
Mirza, Shazia, 104
Mishnah, 180, 214
Morrison, Blake, 237
Moses, 5, 79, 205
Mother Meng, 157

Muhammad, 5, 18–19, 20, 38, 47, 49, 51, 52, 66, 68, 81, 84, 105, 128, 145, 147, 156, 176, 205–7, 210–12, 217, 229, 231–2, 234, 241
Muid al-Din ibn al-Arabi, 192
Muslim Brotherhood, 83
Muslims; see Islam
Myshkin, Prince, 52–3

Nasrudin, 157
Nasty Story, A, 246
New Testament, 4, 79
Nhat Hanh, Thich, 220–1
Niebuhr, Reinhold, 160
Nietzsche, 7
nirvana, 157
Noah, 20

Omar, 112
Old Testament, 39, 70, 79, 193
orderliness, 244

Parable of the Three Servants, 181
Pavese, Cesare, 189
People for the Ethical Treatment of Animals (PETA), 39
Pinocchio, 108
Plato, 115, 117
politeness, 244
Poor Man's Daughter, The, 67
Pope Benedict XVI, 140–2, 160, 194
Pope John XXII, 99
Pope John XXIII, 245

Pope John Paul II, 100, 105, 172–3, 179, 181
Prodigal Son, The, 230
Protestant Reformation, 99
Protestants, 40

Qur'an, 38, 49, 54, 55, 67, 68, 84, 101, 102, 110, 128, 147, 156, 196, 211, 213–5, 231, 233

Rabi'a al-'Adawiya, 191
Rama, 113
Rawls, John, 26, 118–9, 205, 211
Ratzinger, Cardinal Joseph, see Pope Benedict XVI
reincarnation, 60
reliability, 244
Republic, The, 115, 117
Rig Veda, 99, 108
Rivers, Joan, 98
Romeo and Juliet, 188
Rumi, Jalal ad-Din, 139
Ruthven, Malise, 78, 206
Rorty, Richard, 88
Rousseau, Jean Jacques, 119, 177
Rushdie, Salman, 103
Rwanda, 237

Saladin, 231
Satanic Verses, The, 103
sati, 188
Satyagahi, 77, 222
satyagraha, 222
Second Noble Truth, 60
Second Vatican Council, 181
Seinfeld, Jerry, 98

self-discipline, 2, 60–74
Shi'ism, 19–20, 101
shu, 34
Siddhartha, 13–5, 37
simplicitas, 160
Singer, Peter, 41–2, 87, 137, 248
Smith, Wilfred Cantwell, 10
Socrates, 115, 117, 156, 164
Solomon, 166–8, 186
Song of Solomon, 193
St Francis of Assisi, 160
St Paul, 22, 172, 190
Stevenson, Robert Louis, 178–9
Story of Creation, The, 116, 119
Story of Dhat al-Himma, 128
Sufism, 182, 191, 197–8
Sunni, 101
Sun Shuao and the Twin-headed Snake, 50

tact, 244
taqleed, 101
Talmud, 110, 210
Taoism, 131, 143, 179
Tastum, 208
Ten Commandments, 79
Theory of Justice, The, 26
tolerance, 135–53
Tolstoy, Leo, 17, 25, 177, 191, 195, 209–10
Torah, 193
Tragedy of Kerbala, The, 19
Truth of Cessation, 60
Truth of the Path, 60
Tutsis, 237

'Umar Ibn 'Abd al-'Aziz, 16
umma, 82–3
Universal Declaration of
   Virtue, 242–3
UN Declaration of Human
   Rights, 136, 242
untouchables, 40
utilitarianism, 8
Utnapishtim, 16, 25

van Gogh, Theo, 103
Vatican II, 146
virtue
   definition of, 2–3
virtue theory, 8
Virtues Project, 244

Wang Kuo-wei, 196
Wang Yang-Ming, 158, 180
Warraq, Ibn, 103

Weber, Max
Wilson, Gordon, 225
wisdom, 155–69
Wittgenstein, Ludwig, 7, 53,
   88
Woman Caught in Adultery,
   The, 232
work, 171–83

Yom Kippur, 97
Yudhishthira, 85–6, 158–9,
   235
Yusuf, see Joseph

zakat, 54
Zaynu'l-'Abidin, 20
Zen Buddhism, 61, 220, 223
Zi, Sun, 115
Zohar, 193